FLYING FREE
WITH GOD

FLYING FREE WITH GOD

Living in the truth of God's healing love

Tracy Williamson

New Wine Press

New Wine Ministries
PO Box 17
Chichester
West Sussex
United Kingdom
PO19 2AW

ISBN 978-1-905991-26-6

Typeset by CRB Associates, Reepham, Norfolk
Cover design by CCD, www.ccdgroup.co.uk
Printed by Creative Print & Design, Abertillery, UK

CONTENTS

DEDICATION

I dedicate this book to all who long to live in the fullness of what God created you to be, yet feel a part of you is missing or locked away. May you discover the depths of your Heavenly Father's love as He meets with you to heal and set you free.

May you experience the joy of hearing your true name and God-given identity and of learning to live as Royal Son and Daughter.

ACKNOWLEDGEMENTS

So many people have played a part in this book being written, not necessarily through contributing stories, but just through the impact you have had on my life since I became a Christian at nineteen. Thank you, dear friends and church family over the years, who have stood alongside me, loved me, believed in me and prayed for me. Through you I have experienced deep change, healing and release into all that God has called me to be.

Thank you to the many people who inspire me by the quality of their faith and love and their integrity and reality. You have helped me love my Lord more and seek to live my life for Him.

Similarly, thank you to the many authors whose books and writings have had a deep impact on my life. As a deaf person the written word is even more imperative as we cannot hear sermons. Keep going with what you are doing, you writers, because God is working through you to change lives.

Thank you, Patrick, for your valuable feedback. Thank you, Jen, for showing me what God's healing love can do, for being such an inspiration to me in your writing and for setting me on the path of writing myself. Thank you for your wonderfully affirming foreword.

Thank you, Marilyn, you are a constant support and inspiration. Your belief in me has given me the courage to move forward into all that God has for me to be and to do.

Thank you, Mags, for all your wisdom, encouragement and deep understanding over these last four years. The Lord has used you powerfully.

Thank you all my close friends and prayer supporters who have prayed specifically for me and for this book over my months of writing it. Thank you for putting up with my distraction and antisocial reclusiveness through this period! Thank you, all of you who have contributed stories or given permission to quote your words or experiences.

Thank you to Tim Pettingale, my publisher. Your affirmation, trust and acceptance, not forgetting your great patience over these last four years, have given me the ability to move forward in my writing.

Thank you, dear Father, Son and Holy Spirit for your incredible love and transformation; that you make me a new creation – the old has gone, the new has come. May you be glorified through this book.

FOREWORD

Warning! If you want to stay the way you've always been and go on putting up with all your problems, hang ups and hedgehog prickles then close this book quick! It is definitely *not* for you!

On the other hand, if you are fed up with the person you've always been and want to change, but just don't know how, then get stuck in – that is if you are brave enough!

So many of us feel we will always stay permanently damaged because of a difficult childhood, the kind of personality we inherited or the traumatic things which have hit us in the past. In this book Tracy assures us that God is able to heal us completely and transform us into people who can "walk tall" because we know we are loved and highly valued by an adoring Father. Tracy is not just writing about some dry academic theory she has studied, she's lived everything she writes about; it is her own personal experience. Few people I know would dare to do what she has done here, but it is because she has been brave enough to share her own journey towards inner wholeness that this book is so utterly compelling and readable.

I've known Tracy now for many years, both as a close friend and co-worker in the healing ministry. I've seen her changing, growing in grace and confidence as a person; but I've also watched her transforming others who might well have been labelled "No Hopers" into confident, outgoing individuals who radiate peace. So I know that the concepts she writes about in this book have been tried and tested successfully, not only on herself but on many other people, who are now "flying free with God".

When Tracy was a small child a bout of encephalitis left her with poor co-ordination as well as impaired sight and hearing. As she was struggling to adjust to all that, her father died and subsequent abuse of many different kinds made her childhood almost intolerable. "On paper" she ought to be an emotionally disabled adult, but she is possibly the least disabled person I know!

This book takes us all on a journey of discovery as we try to find out, "Who am I, really?" It is quite the most clear, readable and accessible handbook on self-discovery and inner healing that I have ever read, but it is far more than that. It is also a beautifully written devotional book. Interspersed among the narrative Tracy gives us little exercises which help us into a deeper personal relationship with God, and I found the way Tracy kept bringing us, and our pain, back into His presence so moving I cried my way through the whole book!

Tracy has a major problem hearing human voices, but no problem whatsoever in hearing God's voice! In this book she shows us how easy it is for the rest of us to do just that, simply by tuning into Him via the sights and events of our everyday lives. Although she tackles some very painful and difficult issues, her book is actually extremely easy to read, very well written and fast moving. Her startling honestly draws us after her into that deep place of healing. However reluctant we may be to go down into our personal "locked cellar" we feel that if Tracy dared to go there, then maybe we can risk it too.

Jennifer Rees Larcombe

INTRODUCTION

Some years ago at a conference, I was planning what workshops to build into the programme. I felt bored with those we usually offered and wished I could think of something different. Suddenly a phrase popped into my mind: "Meeting with the Father".

"What does that mean?" I thought, rather puzzled. How can I do a workshop on meeting with the Father?

But as I thought about it, excitement began to bubble inside me. The word "meeting" is present tense. Could it be that God had dropped this phrase into my heart, wanting us to create a time where people could meet with and experience Him, rather than just sitting passively listening to teaching?

That moment was the beginning of a session that we have since included in many of our conferences. It is a time of welcoming the Holy Spirit and enjoying the presence of God. Receiving His words of truth through lovely readings and periods of silence to a background of beautiful music. Around the room I place many different symbols: water for cleansing and healing; a wedding ring symbolising us being the Bride of Christ; beautiful blue-green materials representing the streams of living and still waters; a candle; a cross draped in red; a beautiful red royal robe representing the robe of righteousness; a duvet symbolising the deep comfort and compassion with which the Lord wraps us; figures and pictures showing His father, mother and shepherd heart; banners of red, gold and purple to exalt Him as Lord and King; cups and saucers representing Him as our friend...

People move around and touch, look at, wrap themselves in, handle, listen and worship. Each time I am filled with awe as I witness the beauty of God's desire to meet with us, to touch our lives and draw us close to His heart. To speak words of love, affirmation and purpose over us, to open our eyes to see and experience the incredible depth and breadth of the ways in which He makes Himself known to us. Awe fills me too when I hear how people have met with God and experienced healing. One lady, who felt hard and cold in her heart, experienced a wonderful thawing inside as she sat in the duvet of comfort and prayed for God to help her to feel again. A man shared how he was healed of amnesia. A lady who had never married experienced the joy of being the bride of Jesus as she placed the wedding ring on her finger and shared her loneliness with Jesus.

In all of this I sense God's longing for us His children, to truly know Him and for us to live in the intimacy of relationship He offers us. Many of us are caught up in the wounds of life. We know God loves us and has a plan for us, but it is not the way we identify ourselves or live our lives. Hurts and lies cripple our emotions and imprison our spirits. We can feel there is no answer, but in the reality of the Father's love, the death and resurrection of Jesus Christ and the wonderful gift of the Holy Spirit there is every answer. He has always known and loved each one of us and calls us to recognise that and trust our hurting or bound up lives into His hands afresh and to step into the adventure of healing and discovery of how to be and live primarily as His beloved and royal sons and daughters.

I am not writing this book from the finishing line! It is my own adventure as much as yours. In fact, you will discover that a great deal of my own journey of healing and empowering to truly become a Daughter is in these pages. This is not because my story is anymore important than ~ne else's. There are many other people's stories here ~t is simply that I don't want to preach inspiring ~ so much as to share the reality of the journey we ~Just as Jesus openly wept, loved, rejoiced, perienced hunger, tiredness, anguish, agony, and anger, so do we all. And just as Jesus knew thi~ ~n everything that He was the beloved Son of God with a destiny to fulfil, so we too can hear God calling us by the name that brings healing and releasing us to walk in our true destiny as beloved children of God.

Jesus said that His mission was to fulfil the prophetic promise of Isaiah 61:1–3:

> *"The Spirit of the Sovereign LORD is on me,*
> *   because the LORD has anointed me*
> *   to preach good news to the poor.*
> *He has sent me to bind up the broken-hearted,*
> *   to proclaim freedom for the captives*
> *   and release from darkness for the prisoners,*
> *to proclaim the year of the LORD's favour*
> *   and the day of vengeance of our God,*
> *to comfort all who mourn*
> *   and provide for those who grieve in Zion —*
> *to bestow on them a crown of beauty*
> *   instead of ashes,*
> *the oil of gladness*
> *   instead of mourning,*
> *and a garment of praise*
> *   instead of a spirit of despair."*

We cannot come out of inner captivity, grief and despair by our own efforts, but as we look to Jesus and receive His incredible love and healing power we find the impossible becomes not just possible, but our daily experience. Instead of the weariness of heavy weights constantly making us stumble through life (Isaiah 40:30), Jesus gives us hope, joy and strength and releases us to soar with Him on wings like eagles, to fly free, knowing that He is the One who holds us up and will never let us go.

You will see as you travel through the pages of this book that it moves from biblical teaching to personal stories (both my own and others), to times of prayer and suggested personal reflections. All the teaching and reflections are Bible-centred and have also come out of my own journey of prayer, healing and discovery. Don't feel bound to do the reflections, they are not intended to be prescriptive, but simply aim to encourage an open dialogue between us and the Holy Spirit. If you do try them I am sure that God will meet you in them and He will also meet with you in other ways that are just right for you; ways that He opens up as you explore what it means to live in intimacy with your wonderful Father, Friend, Saviour and Lord.

On many occasions throughout the book I refer to the practice of keeping a journal. This is not an onerous, "Got to write something everyday" diary! It is your own personal means of exploring and recording the landmarks in your journey with God. Many people simply use notebooks and write in it as regularly or irregularly as suits them. I personally prefer to use my computer as I find it easier to type than to write. I don't write in my journal every day and some days I may just jot a line about how I am feeling or a verse of the Bible that has blessed me. Other days I may write more, recording how God has met with me, opened my eyes to His love, brought healing or enabled me to hear His voice. Whenever I do any reflective exercises, like those in this book, I jot or type my thoughts down as I do them. Later I have the joy of re-reading how God has touched my life and enabled me to grow or step out in new ways, or simply to see afresh how wonderful He is. It is because of this practice of journaling that I have been able to share many of my encounters with God in this book. If you have never kept a journal, why not have a go? It is for your eyes only, you don't have to worry about spellings in a journal or feel you have to be a polished writer! It is just your own personal way of exploring and recording your unique experience of life and the God who walks it with you.

May you know His joy as you begin this adventure of living in the truth of God's healing love. May you be encouraged and inspired and may this book be an aid to help you further along the path of becoming His beloved child and honoured heir, flying free with God.

Tracy Williamson

flying free
with God

living in the truth of God's healing love

CHAPTER 1

YOU WILL BE GIVEN A NEW NAME

"I will change your name, your new name shall be
Confident, Joyfulness, Overcoming One,
Faithfulness, Friend of God,
One who seeks my face."[1]

A NEW NAME

At a conference recently I was teaching about the importance
of knowing and living in the truth of our new identity in
Christ. I explained how God prophesied through Isaiah that
He would give His people a new name, a name that would
bring healing and transformation (Isaiah 62:2–5). I then

encouraged people at the end of the session to spend a few moments listening to God for their true God-given names.

Later at lunch, I asked the lady sitting opposite me if she had received a new name from God. She shrugged and said, "I don't think so really. An idea did come to my mind, but I think I was just making it up. I didn't think it could have been God, so I ignored it."

When I asked her what it was she very diffidently said, "Well, it was 'Chosen One', but I know that must have just been me."

In that moment of her saying the words "Chosen One" God gave me a vision. It was of a garden centre and God was walking down an aisle with crates of seedlings on either side of Him. Above the crates were pictures of what the seedlings were destined to become: beautiful fragrant flowers. God had a particular one in mind and He was searching for it. In the vision I saw Him stop at a crate and with great joy touch a seedling and look at the picture. He said, "This is it, this is my chosen one, the one that will truly reveal my beauty and fragrance and bring me delight." I knew then that Linda really was that Chosen One, that seedling. The words "Chosen One" were not her imagination. She had truly heard God give her a new name.

I wrote all this down for Linda and passed it over the table to her. She read it and looked stunned then quickly wrote something and passed it back to me. When I read what she had written, I felt stunned too! She wrote that when having some prayer ministry shortly before the conference, the prayer minister had a word for her that she was sure was from God but had no idea what it meant. At the time Linda had no idea what it meant either, so she had pushed it to the back of her mind. Now it made sense. The word given to that prayer minister was: "Garden Centre"!

What a wonderful story showing God's delight in speaking to us and revealing the truth of who we are in Him. He knew Linda's fear, that she was just making things up, and so took care to speak to her in such a way that she would be encouraged, not just that she had been given a beautiful new name, but that she really could hear His voice.

I too was very encouraged as I am never 100% sure that a word or vision really is from God. It was an exciting confirmation that God had been planning to give Linda this garden centre vision way before we had even met. I am sure that when Linda came to share it with the prayer minister who originally had the prophetic word that she too would be encouraged as Linda said she had been very puzzled to receive such strange words!

DESTINED FOR TRANSFORMATION

Recently I was reading the book of Mark and was struck afresh by the dynamic nature of Jesus' encounters with the people around Him. When men, women and children met with Him, there was change and transformation. Broken bodies were healed, broken minds restored, crushed souls made whole. What brought such transformations about? It wasn't simply that Jesus was soft and loving. Some of the things He said or did seemed as gentle as eating nails! Yet there was a catalytic effect, people became different as a result of their meeting with Jesus.

As I reflected on this, a deep awareness opened up in my heart. My relationship with Jesus can never be static. The very fact that I have a relationship with Him at all means that I am living in the process of change and I am destined to become a different person. Not just in the sense that I may do or say different things or have different priorities, or even just that my character is transformed. Jesus brings a much deeper difference. It is a difference of identity. In the core of my being Jesus restores, births and brings to life my new and true identity as the beloved daughter of God and co-heir with Jesus. My life is now a journey to become that daughter and heir in reality. It is a transformation that is both already complete, because of what Jesus accomplished through His death and resurrection, and is also in process. This process requires my partnership. It is a little bit like the process the caterpillar has to go through in order to become a butterfly. Its butterfly nature is already inherent within it, but in order for that to be realised the caterpillar has to go through the process of entering the chrysalis and emerging the other side. If the caterpillar did not enter the chrysalis, its inherent butterfly nature could not come into being. The caterpillar has to actively engage in this process in order to become its new, true self.

The Chrysalis for Us Is Jesus

For us to discover the freedom of flying with our new, beautifully painted wings we have to enter into the chrysalis of intimate relationship with Jesus; into the place where His words become our own words of truth and freedom; the place where His ways of sonship, trust, forgiveness, compassion and power become our own ways; the place where His own Spirit of life comes, infuses and transforms us into His image.

The other day I discovered the original text of Hans Christian Anderson's poignant story *The Ugly Duckling*. It moved me to tears because of its universally needed message of transformation: death to life, ugliness to beauty, hopelessness to joy. Listen with your heart to this extract:

The Ugly Duckling
"Then he flew to the water and swam towards the beautiful swans. The moment they espied the stranger, they rushed to meet him with outstretched wings.

'Kill me,' said the poor bird; and he bent his head down to the surface of the water and awaited death.

But what did he see in the clear stream below? His own image; no longer a dark, gray bird, ugly and disagreeable to look at, but a graceful and beautiful swan...

He had been persecuted and despised for his ugliness, and now he heard them say he was the most beautiful of all the birds. Even the elder-tree bent down its bows into the water before him, and the sun shone warm and bright. Then he rustled his feathers, curved his slender neck, and cried joyfully, from the depths of his heart, 'I never dreamed of such happiness as this, while I was an ugly duckling.' "[2]

PERSONAL REFLECTION

(Use your journal to explore your answers.)

- Do you feel this story has any personal message for you?
- What things in your life make you identify with the duckling's negative view of himself?
- The duckling thought the swans would kill him. If you see the swans in the story as symbolic of God, how do you view their action of "rushing to meet him with outstretched wings"? Deep down do you expect punishment or love from God?
- If you gaze into the pure streams of God's love, what do you expect to see reflected there?
- What does the duckling's joy in discovering he is a beautiful swan instead of an ugly duckling mean to you?

YOU ARE A BEAUTIFUL SWAN

Maybe you have gone through much of your life convinced you are an ugly duckling. Life's rejecting messages, like the pecks, kicks and mockery endured by the duckling have caused you to see yourself as rubbish. But just as the duckling was really a beautiful and graceful swan, so you are made in God's image to reveal His splendour (Isaiah 61:3). God has put a swanlike treasure within you, the unique fingerprint of His beauty.

God made you in His image. Many theological tomes have been written about what this really means. In what way has the image of God been stamped upon us? Is it in our intellect, our ability to create, to reason? Is it something physical or emotional? Is it in our ability to recognise beauty and indeed to create beauty? Is it in our strength and power and ability to lead, control, destroy or build up? Is it that we are communal beings who thrive and grow in relationship just as the Trinity lives in perfect relationship?

I am no theologian. To me all of these factors plus many others are vital elements of being made in God's image, but the key that binds them all together is that God has written into our hearts and minds, bodies and spirits, His capacity to love and to be loved, to know and to be known. Love is the essence of everything that He is and does. Love flowed through His words to bring this Creation into being. Love causes Him to watch over the movements of every tiny sparrow and count every hair on our heads. His heart was broken by love, as we, the height of His creation, chose to ignore His words of life and listen instead to the lies of Satan.

But despite the ugliness of the hatred, lies, brutality, betrayal, selfishness and pain that has gripped our world ever since, God never stopped loving us and has never stopped creating us with the signature of His love written all over us.

Ponder this verse:

"Oh yes, you shaped me, first inside then out, you formed me in my mother's womb . . . My frame was not hidden from you when I

*was being formed in secret and intricately and curiously wrought
as if embroidered with various colours...*"

(PSALM 139:13, 15)[3]

See how David's eyes were opened as he welcomed God's
presence with him. Out of the depths of prayer and thanksgiving he met with God as the Creator who rejoices in
forming His children, sculpting their physical bodies and
delicately painting their characters and spirits with a unique
mix of colours and textures, each one becoming an incredible
treasure.

Jesus too received deep revelation as He spent time
seeking to know His Father and His ways. He saw that the
kingdom of heaven is to do with the heart, God's heart of
passion for us and our heart of love and desire for God.

*"The kingdom of heaven is like treasure hidden in a field. When
a man found it, he hid it again, and then in his joy went and sold
all he had and bought that field."*

(MATTHEW 13:44)

REFLECTION

- Spend some moments imagining the above picture of
  the kingdom of heaven being like treasure found in a
  field. Visualise the beauty of the gold and silver, the
  delicate glory of the sapphires, rubies and diamonds, all
  against the backdrop of a muddy hole in the ground.
- How do you see yourself in this story? Are you that sought
  after treasure or do you imagine yourself as the delighted
  discoverer who sells everything he has to acquire it?
- How does either perspective make you feel?
- Ask God for revelation of all He wants to show you
  through this parable and ask Him if there is any particular
  way you need to apply it in your life.

- Spend time thanking Him that He joyfully gave all He had for you because you are His longed for treasure.
- Worship and praise Him that He is also your treasure, more costly and valuable than anything else in your life.

Do You Know Who You Are?

The Ugly Duckling story is not just about hurts and rejection, but also about not belonging. He didn't match up because he was different. He was a baby swan hatched in a duck's family. He did not fit the niche and role laid down for him. The cruel rejections he experienced all confirmed that deeper pain. Is this a pain you feel? Does your soul cry tears that no one hears but you?

"I don't belong, I'm not all that I should be, I'm not loved for who I am."

Many of us carry such a cry within us. It is an epidemic in our society. We are so busy and outwardly we often strive to look "together", fashionable or cool. But what is really happening on the inside?

I was chatting recently with a young mum and on the spur of the moment I asked her how she was feeling about herself. She replied that she didn't really have any sense of who she was. She didn't know where she was going or who she was meant to be. She just felt a general sense of regret and disappointment in herself.

As I listened to her I felt a growing sadness. So many people have grown up with no real sense of identity. Different roles accumulate in our lives: son/daughter, sister/brother, student, worker, wife/husband, mother/father, Christian worker ... yet these roles, as meaningful as they can be, are not the essence of who we really are. Many have shared about feeling lost, resentful, hopeless or driven by the roles that make up their lives. Roles can often carry hidden messages like stuck on post-it notes. I think of those people I've met: Vivien, crushed by the certainty that her mum and dad really wanted a son; Marilyn, my close friend and ministry partner, driven for many years by the ongoing message from her father that she must do better than everyone else to be accepted. David, battling against the reiterated message that he is stupid, that there's no point in trying because he'll never be good enough. The young wife I met and cried with whose heart ached with shattered dreams, knowing that she is nothing more than her husband's possession. I think of the many young mums who say to me, "I don't work, I'm just a mum!" – a statement full of an underlying sense of being second-best, rather than living out a wonderful purpose in raising their children.

PLEASE TELL ME WHO I AM

We often try our utmost to fulfil our outer roles and ways of identifying ourselves yet inwardly feel something is still missing. Where am I in the midst of all I am doing? Is this role just something I do or is this something I am? Why don't I feel fulfilled when I have so much going for me?

The other day the words of an old pop song by Supertramp kept going round in my mind:

"There are times, when all the world's asleep,
The questions run too deep, for such a simple man.
Won't you please, please tell me what we've learned?
I know it sounds absurd,
But please tell me who I am."[4]

Inside each of us are the haunting questions, "Who am I?", "Why am I here?", "Where am I meant to be going in my life?" The questions are usually buried deep in our subconscious and we get on with our lives, fulfilling our roles and doing the usual things. Yet, as this song expresses, we can find in the quiet of a sleepless night, or when surrounded by people in a social gathering, or at any seemingly irrelevant moment, that suddenly we are gazing into a frightening inner emptiness and confusion.

THE LORD WILL GIVE YOU A NEW NAME

At the beginning of this chapter I referred to one of many similar passages about the wonderful promise of the new name given to us by the Lord as we welcome Him into our lives and receive His salvation:

> *"The LORD will give you a new name. The LORD will hold you in His hands for all to see – a splendid crown in the hands of God. Never again will you be called Godforsaken or Desolate. Your new name will be: God's Delight and The Bride of God, for the LORD delights in you and will claim you as His own ... Then God will rejoice over you as a bridegroom rejoices over his bride."*
> (ISAIAH 62:2–5 NLT, précis)

This promise is addressed to Zion, God's chosen and beloved Holy City. But if we view this as just a national promise and distance ourselves accordingly, we are making a big mistake. In the Bible, God's promises, as indeed His judgements, always operate on more than one level. So this passage, while speaking directly to Zion, was also looking forward prophetically to the new kingdom and nation of believers in Jesus which you and I are a part of.

Viewed purely as a nation and people group, Israel and the Jews hold a dear place in God's heart and have done since the beginning of creation. They will also have a unique part to play in the end time fulfilment of His purposes. Yet that is not the whole story. The very fact that He so often addresses them in human terms gives us the clue to the far bigger picture. God is speaking in these passages to *all* of us who have put our trust in Jesus and thus become both the children and the bride of God. Just as Jesus is the incarnation of God, revealing the fullness of God in human form, so we, if you like, are the incarnation of the Promised Land and the inheritors of God's promises, prophecies and purposes for that land. Because of His incredible love and mercy, we have been grafted in to the original nation.

If you find this hard to absorb in a personal way, then listen to these words from 1 Peter:

> *"But you are a chosen people, a royal priesthood, a holy nation, a people belonging to God that you may declare the praises of him who called you out of darkness into his wonderful light. Once you were not a people, but now you are the people of God; once you had not received mercy, but now you have received mercy."*
>
> (1 PETER 2:9–10)

Peter is writing not just to Jews, but also to the new believers throughout the world. He refers to them amongst other things as "a holy nation". While their old "names" may have been, "Not Belonging", "Not Forgiven", "Not a People", now it is very different. God is naming them, "Chosen", "Royal", "Holy", "A People", "Forgiven" ...

In this we see how Peter has heard the heart cry of God for His people to be joined to Him in close relationship. That has always been God's passion and purpose and it is why in the Old Testament God frequently addressed Jerusalem and the nations of Israel as if they were a person – a beautiful woman whom His heart was yearning over, or a young child that He sought to father and nurture:

> *"When Israel was a child I loved him as a son, and I called my son out of Egypt. But the more I called to him the more he rebelled ... It was I who taught Israel how to walk, leading him along by the hand. But he doesn't know or even care that it was I who took care of him. I led Israel along with my ropes of kindness*

and love. I lifted the yoke from his neck and I myself stooped to feed him."

(HOSEA 11:1–4 NLT)

FAITH HISTORY REFLECTION

I was once given an exercise called a Faith History. I had to reflectively look back over my life asking Jesus to bring to my mind the different ways He had been involved. The leader explained that it didn't matter that I hadn't known Jesus until I was an adult. She said, "He knew you and was constantly working to open your eyes to His love. As you listen expectantly the Holy Spirit will give you revelation of how Jesus was involved in your life from the earliest days."

Somewhat doubtfully I began the exercise. My childhood was not easy and usually, looking back, I could only see painful memories. I sat quietly, thinking of the way those Hosea verses describe His tender, nurturing care. I asked the Lord to show me where He had been in my life. At first, nothing … then little snippets of insight began to come to mind. I suddenly remembered an invisible friend I had when I was very young, and as I prayerfully listened, God said He had been teaching me, even at that early age to believe in and engage with what was unseen. I felt amazed and suddenly excited.

"What else, Lord?" I asked and listened quietly again. I then remembered the corgi puppy my dad bought when I was six whom I named Penny. The Lord showed me how He had helped my dad find her and caused it to be my suggested name that was chosen for her. He knew I needed that sense of significance and I was the only child in my class to have a royal dog! I then saw my mum's desire to give my sister and me nice things and I realised the Lord had been helping me to trust Him as my Provider as I grew older.

Many other snippets of memory came to me, each with a sense of how the Lord had been acting on my behalf. These snippets taught me that there was loveliness in my early life despite all the hard and painful things, because He had been watching over me to open my heart to His love at the right time. At the end of the meditation I felt full of excitement. It had given me a glimpse into aspects of my childhood that I had never thought of before, and I felt deep thankfulness to God for all His acts of goodness throughout my life.

YOUR TURN!
FAITH HISTORY PERSONAL REFLECTION

- Make some time to be undisturbed. Ask the Holy Spirit to open your mind and heart to the truth of God's loving ways and words, to protect you from all lies from the enemy and to draw to your attention to all that God wants to show you.
- Thank Him that He has always known you and been working in your life.
- Spend a few moments reflecting on the Hosea 11 verses then look back over your life allowing any particular ideas or memories to come to mind. Note down any feelings or awareness that comes to you and ask God what He is saying about them and what He wants you to see of Him.
- Continue when you are ready with other memories that come to mind.
- Thank the Lord for what He has shown you and for the way He has been watching over you
- You can do this exercise on several different occasions for different times in your life, so when you feel the time is right to stop, do so and thank Him for all He has been doing in your life.

What Is in a Name?

When I was about thirteen years old, I was walking home from school one day with my best friend. As always we reached the corner of my road first and stood chatting for a while. Somehow we got talking about the meanings of our names. My friend was named after her grandparents and had three Christian names with strong meanings like "Leader", "Pearl" and "Gift of God". She was obviously very proud that her names meant such lovely things.

Rather wistfully I said, "I don't think Tracy has any meaning, it's just a made-up name."

She looked at me and replied,

"To me it seems right that you've got a meaningless name!"

We chatted a few more minutes and then she went home, but I stood staring after her. What had she meant? She had sounded so definite. But surely she didn't think that I was such a meaningless person that I only merited a meaningless name? She was my best friend after all! She must have just meant that I was a free spirit and didn't need to be shackled down with a heavy traditional name!

I tried to comfort myself with this idea and pushed aside the hurt feelings that her comment had stirred up. I soon forgot the conversation, or rather, it disappeared from my conscious memory. But unknown to me it was still lurking in my subconscious. Not in the sense of an indignant, "What right did she have to say that about me?" But deep down I believed it was true! I felt I *was* meaningless and silly. Her comment added to my ingrained self-rejection and I felt shame that when she looked at me she saw what I really was, a meaningless person.

Of course, none of this was really to do with a thirteen-year-old's tactless remark! Many other things were happening in my life, all of which conspired together to rob me of self-worth. On a daily basis I was hearing that I was rubbish, mental and pathetic. Although I became deaf when I was two-and-a-half, it was not fully recognised at school until I was twelve. Not knowing myself that I couldn't hear meant that I had no answer to the constant taunts from my peers and angry exasperation of my teachers. The belief that I was truly stupid and inept was a sick knowing inside me. I felt I was a disappointment and embarrassment and carried this feeling everywhere. Home was no refuge, in fact it was the opposite and as I grew into adulthood it was as if I could feel something essential shrivelling up and dying inside me. My sense of being, my personhood, the me that made me, ME, was gradually curling up, hiding her face and giving up on life.

BEGINNING OF TRANSFORMATION

I have shared in my other books [5] how I finally discovered God's love for me and became a Christian in 1983 at the age of eighteen. A wonderful journey then began; a journey into relationship with God and all the joy, freedom and purpose that brings. I am still on that healing journey today. Step by step, through ministry, counselling and learning to relate to God in a real way, by hearing His voice and doing the things He asks me to do, by receiving the renewing baptism of His Holy Spirit and learning to reach out in the power of His love. Through all these means I have come into a place of deep inner transformation and peace.

And yet, I still hated my name! Every time I had to introduce myself as Tracy I felt silly! As I worked with Marilyn from the age of twenty-one my name was frequently paired with hers when organisers announced us both at the start of a concert. To me, the name "Marilyn Baker" had a real ring to it while Tracy just sounded silly and trite. I knew this aversion to my name was irrational. What is in a name after all? Why did it have such connotations of being pathetic and ineffectual when God had poured so much healing into my life? I knew He loved me, but in the core of my being I could not love myself, because that "self" was Tracy!

I could not get away from the feeling that whenever I told someone my name, I was in effect confessing to being a washout and a failure. None of this was in the form of conscious thoughts. It was just that inside, despite all the healing and change God had brought, deep down I still despised myself and believed negative things about myself. I often joked about my "silly" name with others and started mock competitions to see who could think of the best new name. Temperance, Chastity and Innocence were just some of the suggestions given! But unknown to me, my aversion to my name was not just a fad, but a symptom of a much deeper truth. That while I had let God's love touch and heal so many of my hurts and fears and had thus taken many steps which I would never have thought possible, a deep part of me, the "Tracy part" was still curled up in hiding, unable to believe that she wasn't a mistake and that she was truly wanted and meant to be.

But Wasn't All This Just My Problem?

You may be wondering why I am going into so much detail about my dislike of my name? Wasn't I just a melancholic, depressive kind of personality who couldn't accept myself? Surely this kind of inward struggle isn't relevant to most people who would view themselves in a much more positive light?

Sadly, I don't think that is the case. A great many people I've asked say they don't like their names and wish they'd been called something else. But more importantly, you don't have to dig very far to discover just how much pain and self-dislike so many people are carrying around inside them. Often such feelings are disguised by a bright smile, a serving heart, or even an extrovert, charismatic personality. Yet a secret and vital part of the person is curled up and locked away from life. It is that part that God longs to set free and to heal.

A Little Fun Exercise

(You will need to use your imagination for this and you may like to jot your answers/reflections in your journal.)

- A long-awaited opportunity has arisen for you to meet a much admired famous person (imagine who this might be for you personally – a film star? A Christian speaker? A novelist? A singer? A worship leader? Jesus? Someone who has done something great for others?)
- Watch each person in front of you as they meet the famous person and start to chat. What do you feel as you watch them?
- What emotions are you aware of in your heart as your own turn to meet draws near?
- It is now your turn. See him/her smiling at you and reaching out to shake your hand. What do you feel? When he/she asks you your name how do you feel as you respond?
- As he/she chats with you and asks questions about your life, what is your overriding reaction in sharing about yourself: Pleasure? Happiness? Confidence? Ease? Embarrassment? Shame? Awkwardness? Something else?
- Take some time to reflect over your responses. If your overriding feelings were generally happy ones – excitement and anticipation as the meeting drew near; confidence and ease in giving your name and chatting about yourself, then spend a few moments now thanking the Lord for the person He has made you to be, and that He has enabled you to be relaxed in your own

identity. Ask Him for the grace to see even more clearly who you are and the unique gifts and personality traits He has put in your life that enable you to reflect Him.

- If, on the other hand, your overriding feelings were nervousness, needing to rehearse what to say, embarrassment or shame in giving your name or talking about yourself, then spend a while telling the Lord about it. Don't try to analyse the feelings – maybe you already know why or maybe you have no idea, you just feel you are awkward! Just put it all into God's hands in prayer and tell Him you want to see yourself truly as He sees you and to discover the joy of knowing who you are in Him and being relaxed in that. Thank Him that He wants to bring this about and is able to do it.

- If you have written this in your journal, date the prayer so that in time you can look back and see how the Lord has changed you.

HEARING MY OWN NAME

In a memorable church service a few years ago my pastor shared about the special name that God gives to each of us, quoting the promise from Revelation:

> *"... I will also give him a white stone with a new name written on it, known only to him who receives it."*
>
> (REVELATION 2:17)

My pastor explained that the name God gives us is not just a pretty sounding word but is a powerful life description and enablement to be the person God has created us to be. The God who made us in His own image knows the unique gifts and qualities He has put within us. He gives us a name that both affirms the truth of who we are in Him and empowers us to live in the anointing of the gifts He has put within us.

My pastor had sensed, as he prayed about the service, that God wanted to tell us what our own special names were. This wouldn't be something we could make up or just decide upon. God would give it to us by revelation. He said we should all expect to be able to hear God speaking our names into our hearts and that the revelation might come in different ways to different people because God knows how to get through to each of us. As we listen in expectation then God would draw close and open our spirits up to His presence and enable us to hear Him whispering our names into our hearts.

So along with all the others I went forward and stood quietly listening for God's voice. But although I looked very receptive on the outside, inwardly I was in turmoil, my mind was barraged with the negative names that I had heard so often about myself as I grew up: "Lazy", "Unlovable", "Mental", "Spastic", "Four-eyes", "Perverted", "Stupid". The words burst into my consciousness with all the heaviness of a hammer shattering a window. I felt again the helplessness and shame that I'd constantly felt as a child. It seemed like these words were truly me and I was a fool to think there could be any other name for me. I could hear the taunting voices and felt again the impossibility of being able to do anything to stop them.

I decided to leave the room. But so many people were pressing around me it was difficult to move without disturbing everyone. I didn't know what to do so I prayed in desperation:

"Lord, You know all these negative words filling my mind. They seem to be true, but they're crushing me. I feel confused. I don't know what is You and what isn't anymore. Please let me hear You. If You have a name for me that is different from all these negatives please let me hear it."

As I finished praying, a quietness came over me. I could still "hear" all the negatives, but in a distant way now, as if there was a protective moat all round me. In that quietness I suddenly became aware of another phrase in my mind. How it got there I didn't know as I certainly wasn't thinking along these lines. I was feeling the opposite in every way and yet, here, as gently as if was just the glimmer of an idea passing across my mind, was the phrase *Daughter of Mercy*.

To say I was stunned was an understatement. Could this really be my special name from God? Surely such a beautiful name could not be for me? Yet deep down I knew that God was good and could only speak words of truth and grace. He would never speak to crush and condemn. Even in the wrong and sinful areas of my life His heart would be to Father me and His rebuke would be in kindness and love. His word may pierce like a sharp sword cutting to the root, but would never destroy me. God my creator knew all about me, the truth of who I was and what He had made me to be and what He had dealt with on the cross. Couldn't I receive this beautiful name as truly being from Him? But suppose the words had just been my imagination? Was I pretending something was from God when in reality it was just me trying to make up something nice?

Ponder this injunction:

> *"This day I call heaven and earth as witnesses against you that I have set before you life and death, blessings and curses. Now* ***choose life****, so that you and your children may live."*
>
> (DEUTERONOMY 30:19, emphasis mine)

- We cannot stop negative thoughts hitting us.
- We *can* choose not to believe them.
- Choosing the truth of God leads us from death to life.

In that situation of trying to listen to God while being mentally bombarded with rubbish, I needed to choose to accept the name Daughter of Mercy, as truly being from Him. I couldn't prove He had spoken to me, I needed to accept it by faith. The words had slipped so simply into my consciousness it was easy to dismiss them as my own thoughts. Yet I knew that I would not have thought of them myself. We often feel that God's voice will be very loud and dramatic like a thunderclap. But as He doesn't actually tend to speak to us like that, we then conclude that we never hear His voice as we haven't had such an experience! However, the way that God spoke to Elijah gives us an inkling of the truth that His voice comes in the gentleness of a whisper rather than in the roar of the elements.

> *"After the wind there was an earthquake, but the LORD was not in the earthquake. After the earthquake came a fire, but the LORD was not in the fire. And after the fire came a gentle whisper. When Elijah heard it, he pulled his cloak over his face and went out and stood at the mouth of the cave. Then a voice said to him, 'What are you doing here Elijah?' "*
>
> (1 KINGS 19:11–13)

Just as God was speaking to Elijah as a friend to encourage him and lift him out of his depressive self-absorption, so He comes to us as friend and encourager. His words will always be dynamic and powerful in effect and may well challenge or convict us, or make us deeply uncomfortable as they cut through our deceptions and the masks we hide behind. Yet He speaks as a friend who loves us and as such His words and ways of speaking are gentle despite their power. Francis de Sales wrote, "Nothing is so strong as gentleness, nothing so gentle as real strength."[6] This is a very apt description of the voice and character of God.

Back to the Name!

To return to my story, I knew I needed to receive the name Daughter of Mercy as God's healing truth. My pastor encouraged us to prayerfully reflect on anything that came to our minds and ask God to reveal its meaning and significance. As I prayed I was suddenly filled with joy. I had always struggled with what it meant for me to be a daughter. I had never felt that I truly belonged or had any daughter "rights". Now this name was speaking into that place of deep hurt and emptiness in my life. It was as if God my Father was declaring me to be His daughter and saying that I truly did belong in His family. That I was not a disappointment and that He was proud to call me daughter. It is hard to describe in words the effect of this. In human terms I had so often felt an embarrassment to those around me. No doubt at times this was purely my over sensitive imagination or merited because I was naughty! Yet it had gone very deep. Now, in this moment of listening to God, the word "Daughter" was reaching that wound and bringing it out into the light. It was joy mixed with pain because these were feelings I had buried all my life and it was overwhelming to suddenly have them exposed. Yet I knew, as painful as it was, this was the way of healing and transformation.

The second part of the name, "of Mercy" was also very meaningful. I knew it described the way that Jesus wanted me to reach out to those around me. He had poured His mercy over me in such incredible ways. He loved me and sought me out when I was a mess and had so many negative attitudes and helped me come to know Him. He had worked deeply in my life to bring healing and in the process enabled me to touch the lives of others through the ministry He gave me with Marilyn. Now He was clarifying all that had happened and telling me through this name, Daughter of Mercy, that I was to be someone who gave His mercy away to others, helping them to find it for themselves and so be changed and healed.

A Time to Listen with Expectation

What God did for me in giving me my true name and what He did for Linda (at the start of this chapter) in calling her Chosen One, He also does for you. He loves you and sees the areas of your life where you are hurting and ministers healing in the name He gives you. He knows the plans He has for you and gives you the name that releases you into those plans.

> "... I will also give him a white stone with a new name written on it, known only to him who receives it."
>
> (REVELATION 2:17)

Listening Prayer

- Take time to be quiet and undisturbed.
- Ask the Lord Jesus to protect your mind from all attack from Satan and welcome the Holy Spirit to be your counsellor and to guide you into all truth.
- Pray, "Lord Jesus, I would love to know my true God-given name. Please tell it me in such a way that I can hear and receive it from You."
- Spend time quietly listening. If any ideas/names/words come to you, thank Him and note them down. Don't worry if nothing specific comes at this point. Remember that God has already made clear what many of our true names are in His Word: Daughter, Son, Beloved, Royal Priest, Bride, Branch, Holy Nation, Rock ... Prayerfully reflect on these and any other scriptural names you can think of. If any seems particularly significant, note it

down and thank Him for it. Ask Him to enlarge your understanding of what it means.

- Reflect on what has happened. If any particular hurts or memories have been stirred up, tell Him about them and entrust them to Him to deal with.
- Spend time worshipping and thanking Him for the truth He is speaking into your life.

Notes

1. *I Will Change Your Name* by D.J. Butler, © 1987, Mercy Publishing/ Vineyard.
2. *The Ugly Duckling* by Hans Christian Anderson, 1844.
3. Psalm 139:13 (MSG); v. 15 (AMP).
4. 'The Logical Song' by Supertramp from the album *Breakfast in America*.
5. *Expecting God to Speak to You*, © 2005, *Letting God Speak Through You*, © 2006, *Encountering God*, © 2007. All published by New Wine Press.
6. St Francis de Sales quotes (French Roman Catholic bishop of Geneva, active in the struggle against Calvinism, 1567–1622).

flying free with God

living in the truth of God's healing love

CHAPTER 2

THE JOURNEY TO BECOMING

"He takes all our sinfulness and gives to us His holiness.
We've become the sons and daughters of the King."[1]

SONS AND DAUGHTERS OF GOD

I was walking Pennie, Marilyn's guide-dog around our local field. It is a walk I do daily and it isn't really very inspiring! The field is no place of compelling scenery, it is simply a big square of trampled down grass with a muddy walkway round the edge. But it is convenient being only a minute's walk away from our home.

On this particular day it was frosty but a heavy, dark day and I wanted to get home quickly. As I turned the top corner

41

I glanced back. In that moment, very unexpectedly, the clouds parted and sunlight poured through, transforming the frosty field into a glittering golden sea.

I stopped, transfixed by the sight. Stillness hung over everything as if creation itself was holding its breath, marvelling at the beauty. Nothing stirred. Even Pennie stood quietly at my side.

I could hardly breathe. Something momentous was about to happen. I knew that God was there, His presence was overwhelming. It was no accident that the sun had lit up the frost in such a dramatic way just as I happened to be looking. I waited expectantly, awed by the beauty before me.

Usually such moments are gone in a flash, but seconds ticked by and still the fiery gold lit up the field. It was amazing that something ordinary and boring had been transformed into something so glorious. As I prayed I became aware of a verse running over and over in my mind:

"The creation waits in eager expectation for the sons of God to be revealed."

(ROMANS 8:19)

This was the key. The field, when touched by the golden rays of the sun, had been transformed from its ordinary state into something glorious. In that moment of awareness God whispered into my heart: *"I have shown you this as a picture of what you and all My sons and daughters truly are in Me. You and so many others see yourselves as boring, ineffectual and ordinary, but My glory is within you and upon you. And creation itself, this world and all the people that inhabit it, is waiting for that glory to be revealed. There will be no limit to what I can do in this world when My sons and daughters rise up in their true God-given glory."*

With that, the clouds massed together again. The sun disappeared as quickly as it had come out and the field returned to normal. But as I completed my walk I could not forget what I had seen and its spiritual message. The sense of awe filled me over the next few days. God had come close. He had turned an everyday task in a very ordinary location into a sacred moment, a meeting with the Eternal. Yet as profound as this was for me personally, I knew that it was for more than my ears. There were several dynamic elements to that experience, each of which could have the effect of a key unlocking doors in our lives, enabling us to both see and live in a new dimension in our relationship with God.

- God *wanted* to speak to me and share His heart with me.
- God came alongside me in an ordinary place while I was doing an ordinary task.
- God acted and spoke through creation in such a way that I was compelled to stop, look, worship and listen to Him.
- God revealed the glory He has given to us, His children.
- It is vital that we accept and live in the truth that He has made us His glorious sons and daughters.
- Through this truth a door will open in the created world for God's works and power to be powerfully manifested through us, His sons and daughters.
- Creation is waiting for this. How long are we going to make it wait?

We are His glorious sons and daughters. Let's think specifically about two of these key statements:

- God revealed the glory He has given to us, His children.
- It is vital that we accept and live in the truth that He has made us His glorious sons and daughters.

How Do We View Ourselves?

God said to me in that field experience that although we may view ourselves as ordinary or boring, we are actually covered and indwelt by His glory. The field was just ordinary grass until transformed by the golden fire of the sun. We need to see with eyes of faith that God has taken what is ordinary, even marred in us, and exchanged it for something beautiful, His own righteousness and glory. It is a glory our world desperately needs to experience, the glory of becoming the beloved children of God able to know Him and to do His wonderful works of love.

Marilyn and I travel around a lot and often stay in people's homes. I am always interested to see how children relate to their parents and their home life. Are they relaxed and at ease in their own homes? Can they chat with their parents? Can they be themselves or do they have to fit a mould? The answers vary from family to family. I remember once how I felt close to tears when sharing an evening meal with a family and saw how much interest and attention the father paid to his son as he chatted about his day at school. Not all the son said was very sensible, but the dad listened as if his words in that moment were all that mattered. Something stirred in me then, a deep hurt that this had not been my own experience. Meal times in my family were usually fraught, tense affairs. We ate in silence as quickly as we could. Any unlooked for comments were jumped on, anger just a hairsbreadth away. To chat about inconsequential things was an impossibility; to have loving attention from a father figure beyond imagining.

My illness had made me quite clumsy and I was always in a state of nervous dread lest I spilt something or banged a knife or a glass too loudly on the table. I remember how, years later when working with Marilyn, we stayed with an elderly couple, John and Ivy. I accidentally broke a wine glass spilling its contents everywhere. Everything seemed to freeze as if time had stopped. I went rigid, already hearing in my mind the frenzy of anger. I must have closed my eyes and I jumped when I felt a light touch on my arm. When I saw John smiling and offering me a fresh glass of wine something broke inside me. I began to cry and couldn't stop. The poor couple were alarmed at my reaction to something which to them was nothing to worry about: "It's only a glass!"

God used their simple loving kindness and, on the previous occasion, the carefree chatting of the young boy with his dad, to reach into a locked place of my life; a place where I had no idea how to be daughter. He gave me windows into what true sonship/daughtership can be. Here are the names of some of those windows:

- The right to be who I am and to share it without fear.
- The joy of knowing that what I say is valued and listened to even if it isn't right.
- That it is a good and natural thing for social occasions to be times of loving togetherness.
- I don't have to hide my weaknesses. I am accepted as "me".

OFTEN OUR WINDOWS ON TRUTH HAVE BECOME BLURRED AND DISTORTED

I had a friend once called Susan.[2] Susan and her sister, Jane, were very different. While Jane was relaxed and confident in herself, Susan was full of fear. She would never look me in the eye; she shrank away from every hug, her very movements were stiff and clumsy as if her body was locked in a cage. If I asked her opinion on anything she could never bring herself to respond. I grieved for her and puzzled over why Susan should be so bound when her sister was so free. It obviously wasn't her upbringing because she had told me herself what loving parents she had. When I gently tried to probe into why she was so afraid, she told me it was just her, she was a bad person and she knew it. I asked her what her mum and dad were like and she was adamant they were good and loving parents. I had to leave it there but the questions remained. I was very fond of her and longed for her to be free.

Some years later I found out the truth from someone who knew the family. Her parents were indeed loving – to her sister! Jane was wanted and much loved, their princess. They had not wanted another child, but if they did have one it had to be a boy. Susan was a disappointment and they never let her forget it. Seeing how much they lavished love on her sister made Susan believe a terrible lie about herself, that she was bad and deserved every cruel word she got. Whatever anyone said to her to the contrary, she was convinced of her own badness. But throughout all those years of knowing her, even hearing how good her parents were, I could not shake off the question: *If her parents were so wonderful, why is Susan so damaged?*

REFLECT

Bearing in mind those "windows" God began to open into my need to be daughter, what kind of windows do you think Susan needed opening in her life? One idea comes immediately to my mind. Add your own thoughts here too:

- God made her and lovingly created her female. She was not a disappointment to Him.
- ....
- ....
- ....

NOW WELCOME THE GENTLE YET PIERCING LIGHT OF JESUS INTO YOUR OWN HEART

- Do you identify in any way with either of these stories?
- Do the windows of sonship/daughtership already described gel with you at all?

- Are you aware of any ordinary occasions when you have felt opened up or have overreacted?
- In prayer ask the Lord if there are other windows He needs to open up into your understanding of yourself as a child and Him as your Father.
- Thank Him that He loves you and is working within you to bring healing. Tell Him you want to be free to choose to start believing His truth about yourself and to renounce the lies of the enemy.

GOD LONGS FOR US TO DISCOVER HIS FATHER LOVE

God longs for us to discover His Father love and for us to live in the truth of what that means, that we *are* His beloved children. Unlike the tragic truth about Susan's parents, there is no deception in God. He cannot show love to one and not to another. Saul was an accessory to murder and was actively and dangerously seeking to destroy the new church. Yet God deliberately sought Saul out. He confronted him with His holy power on the road to Damascus and inflicted blindness on him. Yet rather than being cowed, Saul was transformed and filled with awe and love for God. He never forgot that he had been the *"worst of sinners"* (1 Timothy 1:16), yet that knowledge just made him full of joy as he exalted in God's grace and incredible forgiveness. He never grovelled in a self-abasing way but was happy to simply affirm and live in his new identity, symbolised by his name becoming Paul instead of Saul. He begins every letter with a simple declaration of who he is now, the truth of what God has made him to be in His kingdom.

> *"Paul, an apostle – sent not from men nor by man, but by Jesus Christ and God the Father..."*
>
> (GALATIANS 1:1)

Identifying himself in this way, Paul is living out the truth that he passionately teaches:

> *"Therefore, if anyone is in Christ, he is a new creation; the old has gone, the new has come . . . God made him who had no sin to be sin for us, so that in him we might become the righteousness of God."*
> (2 CORINTHIANS 5:17, 21)

Paul also wrote to the Romans:

> *"You did not receive a spirit that makes you a slave again to fear, but you received the Spirit of sonship. And by him we cry, 'Abba, Father.' The Spirit himself testifies with our spirit that we are God's children . . . heirs of God and co-heirs with Christ."*
> (ROMANS 8:15–17)

YOU RECEIVED THE SPIRIT OF SONSHIP . . . THE SPIRIT HIMSELF TESTIFIES WITH OUR SPIRIT . . .

Maybe you have grown up feeling crippled in your understanding of what it means to have a Father who loves you unconditionally, who seeks you out and lavishes His love on you so that you become His beloved child. Maybe you have been told you are loved, but the message has come in packaging that's left you guilty and striving to do everything right, or perhaps shamed and confused about what love really is.

SHAMED AND CONFUSED

I carried such shame and confusion since the first time I was told I was loved while being forcibly touched where no one should touch a young girl. I hated it and it made me sick inside. But always there were the words, "You know I love you." I fought, but then came more angry words, "You're perverted, why can't you be normal?"

It was my fault. Was it true I was perverted? Is this what the girls at school were always talking about, but which I could never quite hear? Was this love? Confusion and fear took over. There was no one I knew that I could ask. I didn't know what to say – it was all me – my guilt, my shame. But one thing I knew, if this was what being a woman meant I didn't want it.

Shame makes you hide away. I curled up on the inside and set the barriers high so no one could see in. I did all the usual teenage things and threw myself into my schoolwork. No one knew what was happening inside me. I wasn't even sure myself! What I did know was that as I got older the constant ache of confusion about my femininity squeezed my heart shut. I locked my girlish hopes and dreams in a box and endured the years of growing emptiness.

What I didn't know, and what none of us realise when going through such times of deep pain, was that God was watching over me with such yearning love, working to bring me to that point of knowing Him and to the joy of discovering that the Tracy I had locked away was safe in His hands and His resurrection life would bring her to life again.

GOD CHOSE US BEFORE HE MADE THIS WORLD TO BE HOLY AND BLAMELESS

There is a verse which stopped me in my tracks when I first discovered it in the words of a song we were singing at church. I'd been a Christian for a few weeks but was struggling, even though I now knew God loved me. The verse says:

"Praise be to the God and Father of our Lord Jesus Christ …
For he chose us in him before the creation of the world to be holy
and blameless in his sight."

(EPHESIANS 1:3–4)

I remember we sang these words over and over as was the fashion in my church, a lively Christian Fellowship. Usually I felt irritated, wanting to move on to other songs, but this time it was as if the meaning of those words was cracking a wall inside me. Surely it couldn't be true that He'd chosen *me*? To be *holy*? How could that be? My first reaction was anger! I'd shown no anger for years and suddenly now I wanted to shout and scream in the middle of worship! But deeper even than the anger was the piercing of longing and hope. This was God, not man we were singing about. Could it possibly be that His love for me was true? Could I dare to believe what He said about me?

GOD WALKS WITH US IN OUR PAIN AND TALKS US THROUGH TO PEACE

Those questions I asked myself: "Could it possibly be?", "Could I dare to believe?" are the starting point of healing. Recognising and owning the fact that we do have longings, even if buried for many years, opens the door for Jesus to come in. And Jesus longs to do that so much. I think of Peter after he disowned Jesus three times. The Bible says succinctly, *"he* [Peter] *went outside and wept bitterly"* (Luke 22:62). In that moment, shame and remorse gripped Peter. The bitter tears revealed his state of heart. He had come face to face with his own worst enemy: himself. And he could neither forgive nor let go of what he had done. Similarly, when we are hurt or have hurt others, we cannot easily forgive or let go. The pain holds us too tightly and deep down the fear of not even having that pain as our identity can be too strong. And yet buried underneath all these locked doors of confusion are hope and longing to find Jesus. We see this with Peter when Jesus met the

disciples on the shore after they'd spent all night unsuccess-
fully fishing:

> *"As soon as Simon Peter heard* [the disciple] *say, 'It is the
> Lord,' he wrapped his outer garment around him and jumped
> into the water."*
>
> (JOHN 21:7)

This action was the voice of Peter's hope and longing for
Jesus. We all have that voice within us. It can rise up in the
middle of a song like it did with me in church, or through a
preacher's turn of phrase, someone's testimony, or something beautiful we see...

Jesus then singled Peter out and deliberately talked him
through his pain and guilt and deliberately re-commissioned
him to service in the kingdom (v. 15). The way of healing is
not easy. In love, Jesus compelled Peter to face what he had
done and to make fresh choices to undo those sins. He
offered Peter love and honour, but Peter had to choose to
receive that and make it his "now" identity: *"Lord, you know
that I love you!"* In making that choice and trusting that what
Jesus said was true, Peter was able to break free of the devil's
bonds of condemnation and stand afresh in the love and
purpose of God for his life.

For me, that night in church was the beginning of my
emerging from the pain cocoon. As with Peter I found that
Jesus would not let me go but sought me out in my hiding
places! Again and again over the next few years He brought
me the double-sided coin of needing to forgive others and
to forgive myself; needing to renounce the lies of the enemy
and to believe the truths of God; needing to face my own
buried pain and to recognise that Jesus was tenderly holding
me; needing to break my protective, cynical habitual
reactions and to step out in the love-commissioning Jesus
gave me.

You Received the Spirit of Sonship ... the Spirit Himself Testifies with Our Spirit ...

As I think again of Paul's words to the Romans, hope bubbles up. Paul declares that we have been given both the means of being God's children and of knowing in an ongoing way that we truly are that. You have been given the *Spirit* of sonship, the Holy Spirit. You don't have to work up "being a child of God", you just have to receive it. All you need is to recognise that through the Holy Spirit of Jesus coming into your life, He has brought you a most amazing gift – the gift of being the child of God. The Holy Spirit confirms within our hearts that we are truly God's children. At His baptism, when the Holy Spirit rested on Jesus in the form of a dove, Jesus heard the voice of His Father God declaring that He was God's beloved Son (Matthew 3:17). Paul is inviting us to expect to hear the same Spirit of God speaking the truth deep into our own hearts that we too are the beloved children of God.

Ponder these verses from 1 John:

> *"How great is the love the Father has lavished on us, that we should be called children of God! And that is what we are!"*
>
> (1 John 3:1)

I love the phrase: *"And that is what we are!"* John is full of joy. He has received revelation about his own sonship. He knows that his name is "Son" and all because of God's incredible love for him. John is urgent that we know this too. He cries out to us to see the greatness of God's love in making us His children. We so often focus on our sense of failure and even feel it is very Christian to do so! Are we not sinners, lost in darkness without God? We may now be saved by grace, but still we are basically sinners needing forgiveness. The aim of our lives is not that *we* are seen but that God is.

This understanding of ourselves purely as sinners constantly needing God's grace is so entrenched in much of the Church that we often accept it without thinking. Yet does this view really glorify God?

SINNERS OR SONS?

The other week I felt very upset with myself for failing in my commitments. Each night I went to bed feeling guilty and calling myself a loser. I said to the Lord as I lay in bed one night, asking Him yet again to forgive me:

"I'm never going to break free of this pattern of failure."

Immediately this thought came to me:

"That's because you're spending all your time looking at your failures. If you looked at Me instead and focused on all that I am and on My love for you then you would break free. You become what you look at."

YOU BECOME WHAT YOU LOOK AT

I was amazed by this thought. I knew it must be from God and it made so much sense. It was true that I had been focusing very much on my failure. My sense of past failure meant that every time I came to tackle a job I was gripped by the feeling that I was bound to fail yet again. Now God was calling me to look to Him, to spend time mulling over in my mind what He is like, dwelling on it, painting a picture of His character and ways. I used to joke in my pony-mad teen years that those who spent all their time around horses, often ended up looking like horses themselves! But I had never applied this to my relationship with God!

You may say from that story: "Well doesn't that just show that we should be looking at God not at ourselves?

Yes that is true! But in what way was God counselling me to look at Him? He was telling me to get my focus off my failures and belief that I would never change and to look instead at His love *for me*. He wanted me to bask in His love, to enjoy it, to recognise in deeper and deeper ways that to love and to restore us is His character and delight. As Paul expresses in his prayer for the Ephesians:

> *"And I pray that you, bring rooted and established in love, may have power, together with all the saints, to grasp how wide and long and high and deep is the love of Christ,* **and to know this love that surpasses knowledge** *– that you may be filled to the measure of all the fullness of God."*
>
> (EPHESIANS 3:17–19, emphasis mine)

BUT HOW DO WE LOOK AT GOD?

The other evening some friends brought round their three-month-old son. As Sarah lifted baby Daniel and gently put him in my arms I was moved by the glow of pride and love in her expression. She stroked his head, laughing that it looked like he was going to have her red hair, and was obviously delighted in him. As I cuddled him I saw how he was constantly looking around for his mum and dad and was so happy when he made eye contact, reaching out his hands to touch their faces.

It was a lovely encounter, but after they left I couldn't forget it. I felt that God was speaking to me through it:

> *"I gave you that encounter with Ben and Sarah and little Daniel as a picture, a way for you to meet with Me and discover My heart of love and delight in My children and a way for you to see how much joy it brings Me when you as My child look to make contact with Me and reach out for Me."*

Pause to ponder...

Are you willing to let a moment in life like that become a mirror that God holds up to your heart?

This experience became a beautiful moment of revelation – seeing God as the delighted parent, we as the loved child reaching out happily to his mum or dad. It moved me and also made me look into my heart with these questions:

- Do I see God as looking upon *me* with this kind of delight and pride?
- Am I like baby Daniel? Do I look out for God? Do I want to touch Him? Am I expectant of making contact with Him?

Let these be your questions too. It may be you have your own children or like me, enjoy times with families or friends who have children. Let them be a picture to you as you reflect. Don't try to answer in a "right" way, answer from your heart response. If it helps, write it in your journal as it may be important to explore afterwards what your answer means to you.

Experience life with an expectation that God wants to make Himself known through the ordinary things around you.
The experience with Daniel and his parents encouraged me in quite another sense too. I felt moved by seeing the family. It seemed significant in some way and as I listened God spoke. This whole process revealed a key that is vital for our journey to become true Son's and Daughters of God. God speaks to us and reveals what He is like through His Word and the ordinary things around us becoming windows into His heart. He gives us revelation of His character and opens the door of longing in our hearts to find and to know Him. That knowing, in turn, works deep within us to bring to life the true picture of who we are in Christ.

WINDOWS INTO GOD'S HEART

In Luke 15 Jesus describes a whole series of pictures from everyday life, all revealing the tender-hearted care of His Father in seeking out those who are lost. The stories are graphic yet startlingly simple. Why did Jesus teach like this? Two reasons come to mind. First, stories are an extremely powerful way of enabling us to connect both with God and with ourselves, and second, with each story Jesus preaches a hidden, mind-boggling sermon:

"Live life, love life, look at life, hear God and experience healing."

Jesus made a choice at the age of twelve to "be in His Father's house" and to seek to grow in His understanding and knowledge of God above everything else, even the expectations of His earthly parents (Luke 2:49). That choice became His way of life. Not in the sense of always being in the temple, but in that He had a passion to see His Father God, to hear His words and to become like Him. As He went from place to place, staying with families and sharing in the day-to-day struggles and joys of living, the heart and purposes of His Father were revealed to Him. Again and again He expressed through His teaching and stories how ordinary things of life can become windows into God's heart and ways.

THE PRODIGAL SON

One of these windows was Jesus' incredible story of a father who gave his wayward son the cash and freedom he demanded, even though he knew full well how his son would use it. And then, after years of patiently waiting and grieving, he accepted him back, not to a life of judgement and slavery as the son fully deserved, but restored to the full status of beloved son and heir.

"But while he was still a long way off, his father saw him and was filled with compassion for him; he ran to his son, threw his arms around him and kissed him.

The son said to him, 'Father, I have sinned against heaven and against you. I am no longer worthy to be called your son.'

But the father said to his servants, 'Quick! Bring the best robe and put it on him. Put a ring on his finger and sandals on his feet. Bring the fattened calf and kill it. Let's have a feast and celebrate. For this son of mine was dead and is alive again; he was lost and is found.' So they began to celebrate."

(LUKE 15:20–24)

This story flew in the face of all that was taught about God's holiness and divine right to judge. Jews thought of God as "Lord God" and "Mighty King", not as the Father who embraces His sinful children and throws a banquet for them! How did Jesus have this understanding of God as a tender Father? We cannot know for sure, but I believe that, amongst other things, as Jesus grew up He observed His own father's character and ways. We know that Joseph was a just and kind man who truly loved God and acted as protector over his family. Through all Jesus' formative years He would have seen a true picture of fatherhood in his dad. More importantly, Jesus knew and loved His Heavenly Father and as He listened to Him and opened up His spirit to Holy Spirit revelation, the true understanding of the power and love of God's Father heart enthralled and empowered Him.

It is obvious too that Jesus loved the Scriptures and spent much time meditating on them, constantly seeking to grow in His understanding of what they really meant. Even at twelve years old, the learned religious leaders were astounded by the questions He asked and the insights He spoke out. He was prepared even then to let the revelations God gave Him into Scripture take Him beyond the accepted view of God.

Pause to ponder...

- Has anyone in your life ever shown you what love, kindness and integrity really are? Have you ever asked God to give you revelation of what He is like through what you've seen in this person?
- Do you expect the Holy Spirit to give you revelation and understanding of God's character and your own place in His heart?
- As you read Scripture, do you expect that He might reveal things to you to deepen your understanding of God, maybe even different things to what you've always experienced in your Christian tradition?

Meditating on Scripture is a key to us receiving God's transforming and healing power.

The Word of God is powerful and effective. It is never just words, but spirit and life. We can imaginatively become part of a story like that of the prodigal son, seeing ourselves as one of the characters, and asking God to give our innermost being revelation of what it means. I did this with this very story when at a retreat centre some years ago. They had a room with Rembrandt's beautiful picture *The Return of the Prodigal Son* covering one wall. I sat opposite the picture with the story before me. I had been feeling really low, struggling with painful memories that were giving me such a deep sense of shame and fear that I wondered if I was truly a Christian.

The picture portrays the old father tenderly embracing the bedraggled and shamed prodigal kneeling at his feet. It is very poignant. As I gazed, all I could think of was the incredible tenderness of the father. I felt such an ache inside to know His tender love holding me like the father in the picture held his son. Suddenly I became very aware of God in the room with me, making the story and the picture my own experience; as if I were the prodigal son, shamed, dirty, yet lovingly embraced and accepted. It was so real, so overwhelming. Hardly thinking, I tried to jot down what I was experiencing. Later I read it and realised I had never before experienced God in such a deep way. But the wonderful thing is that the cleansing I describe in my writing was real. Something shifted and changed inside me as a result of that experience. I know that whatever the enemy may try to do to bind and rob me, I am forgiven, loved and accepted by God. All this had come about as I prayerfully meditated on a Bible passage. This is what I wrote:

A Father tender, You reach down to me.
You see all the filth and shame
But You look at me.
You look at me, for me
You look into me
Calling me to look into You.
So long You have looked for me,
Patient, waiting,
Yet full of yearning love.
You reach out to touch me
And I shrink back, but
You are a Father tender.
"Let Me hold you, draw you close," You whisper
Momentarily I cry out, so full of fear,
But You are a Father tender.
You draw me into Your arms
And I feel Your power
So strong, yet so gentle.
O Father, never have I been held
So tenderly, cherishingly.
How can You, Creator of all
Be so incredibly tender?
I draw back to see Your face and in so doing

See that I have left an imprint of my dirtyness upon
    Your white robe.
I feel horror and gaze at You
Only to be melted by Your smile of such deep love and
    understanding.
You look down at Your breast where that stain has
    come
And it is as if it becomes words that You can read and
    understand.
And I see tears in Your eyes,
Great pools of tears,
And they flow down and over Your breast and all the
    stain is gone.
You shine white, pure, beautiful again.
And me? Even as I watch
I feel a rushing cleansing in my own breast.
I look down and to my amazement
My filth is gone too and I am clothed
In the same radiant beauty as You.
Incredulous I gaze at You
And I see Your joy,
Even the twinkle in Your eye
At my amazement.
I am filled with awe at You.
I love the way You Father me.[3]

THE PROPHETIC IMPORT OF THE STORY

The story of the prodigal son, his radically loving father and
duty-bound elder brother is weighty in prophetic meaning. I
believe that in this day God is opening our eyes in a new way
to the reality of how we have been living as His sons and
using His resources. The story typifies two forms of slavery,
both of which stand opposed to God's Kingdom of grace
and love:

1. The slavery of condemnation

> *"I have sinned against heaven and against you. I am no longer worthy to be called your son."*
>
> (LUKE 15:21)

2. The slavery of joyless duty

> *"All these years I've been slaving for you and never disobeyed your orders. Yet you never gave me even a young goat so I could celebrate with my friends."*
>
> (LUKE 15:29)

Are you bowed under the slavery of condemnation? Like that younger son you know you have messed up, you've hurt people, and you've thrown away good opportunities, you've squandered resources and made choices that fill you with regret.

Or is it that you have been "doing your bit" in church for years? You've given your time and your money. You've read your Bible and prayed. You've attended all the church committees and made teas and coffees whenever it's your turn. But you have no sense that God loves you. You've never seen Him working on your behalf, only for others. Deep down you feel He just takes what you can give Him. Instead of joy you are full of disappointment and resentment of those who seem happy in their faith. You are the slave of duty.

Whichever our form of slavery, God wants to release us. His Kingdom is not to do with condemnation, fear or duty, but grace, love and power. In all the years of living and working with him, neither son had taken time to *see* him. As a result neither son knew their rights and riches as dearly loved sons and heirs. In that moment of the prodigal's return there was a colossal paradigm shift as both sons came face to face with the truth.

As I pray and write God is putting this story prophetically

and powerfully on my heart that this is His purpose for His Church in this day:

- This is the day when I will cause My children to see and own where they have been in their hearts.
- I will draw them to return to Me and to see Me as I am.
- They will speak out of their enslaved woundedness, but will find My embrace.
- I will clothe them with royal robes and place My ring of authority on their hands.
- They will lay down their yokes of slavery and discover the joy of celebration.
- They will step out of poverty into the knowledge that "All I have is theirs".

Prayer

"Father, forgive me for every way I've failed to see Your Father heart and therefore failed to see myself truly as Your beloved child. Cleanse and release me from all 'slave' mindsets and help me to step forward into all You have for me. Thank You for your patient and watchful love over me. Let me be clothed with You. Let me discover what it means to celebrate with You. Thank You that all that You have is mine – that is incredible and mind-boggling. Please empower me and transform me by Your Holy Spirit as I move on in my 'journey to becoming' not just a Son/Daughter, but a co-heir with Christ. Amen."

Notes

1. 'O Lord, You Are So Mighty' by Marilyn Baker from the album *Face to Face*, © 1992, Word UK.
2. Susan's name changed for confidentiality.
3. *The Father Tender* by Tracy Williamson. 9th October 2004 at Loyola Hall in the Rembrandt room looking at the picture of the prodigal son embraced by the father.

flying free
with God

living in the truth of God's healing love

CHAPTER 3

THE BURIED
CHILD

"And like a child I will dance in Your presence
Oh, let the joy of heaven pour down on me."[1]

IT'S NOT JUST RUBBISH!

Recently I watched one of those reality TV programmes. This particular one was putting refuse collectors in the spotlight. One of the men expressed his amazement at the things people throw away. The camera filmed him pulling a lovely necklace from a sack and a completely undamaged glass ornament. In another sack there was a nice blouse. Everything was covered in gunge from the bins, but the items in themselves were like little treasures. As I watched I felt a deep sadness.

"Lord, is this sadness from You?" I asked.

As I prayed I realised that the treasures pulled from the bins were like the treasures of childhood that we so often bury. We bury painful memories, for example; memories of being mocked or abused. But with those memories we also bury our childlikeness – our innocence, curiosity, wonder and trust in life, people and goodness. We may even make a vow that we will never show our vulnerable real selves again. All these are the treasures that get thrown out with the rubbish.

Frances Dewar writes about this buried treasure:

> "There lies within each of us a treasure chest covered in barnacles, half buried in silt, like an old box at the bottom of the sea that no one would look at twice. But inside is a very precious stone, that is to be brought out, shaped and polished, it is to be a gift to enrich others."[2]

It may not be that anything particularly bad happened in childhood, but sometimes just the way our culture interprets what growing up means and pressurises us from an early age to conform, makes us bury everything that seems different from the norm.

The Logical Song quoted earlier says:

> "When I was young it seemed that life was so
>   wonderful
> A miracle, oh it was beautiful, magical
> And all the birds in the trees
> Well they'd be singing so happily
> Oh joyfully, oh playfully watching me.
> But then they sent me away to teach me how to be
>   sensible
> Logical, oh responsible, practical
> And they showed me a world where I could be so
>   dependable

Oh clinical, oh intellectual, cynical.
There are times when all the world's asleep
The questions run too deep for such a simple man
Won't you please, please tell me what we've learnt
I know it sounds absurd
But please tell me who I am...[3]

Learning to close our eyes to wonder and mystery; dismissing beauty as science, love as chemistry and God as an irrelevant crutch means in effect we are closing our eyes to our own selves. It is then that the cry comes in the night, "Who am I? What is the point of *me*?"

PUTTING CHILDHOOD BEHIND US?

The tragedy is that although of course we must grow into maturity as adults, the essence of who we are, the way we experience life, love, beauty, work, family and the joy of relationship with God is all written into our make-up. The way we learn and develop our minds is unique, the things that inspire and move us to be creative, to love and be able to make rich and lasting friendships. Those who love sport or dance and know the exhilaration of such incredible physical control and creativity have that woven into them by God.

As God said to Jeremiah when He called him into ministry,

"Before I formed you in the womb I knew you,
 before you were born I set you apart;
 I appointed you as a prophet to the nations."

(JEREMIAH 1:5)

God does not have favourites! This word to Jeremiah is true for you too. You were known to God before He formed you. In the womb He delighted in weaving together all the strands of your personality, mental and physical abilities, emotional treasures and spiritual pathways. He set you apart for a special purpose. Jeremiah's purpose was to be a prophet to the nations, but this would not just land on him out of the blue. Instead, all the special gifts and character traits he would need to fulfil that purpose were growing in him from conception and being developed throughout childhood. But Jeremiah, like many of us, viewed his youth as something negative and disqualifying. God, however, saw it differently:

> " '*Ah, Sovereign* LORD', *I said, 'I do not know how to speak, I am only a child.'*
> *But the* LORD *said to me, 'Do not say, "I am only a child."* ' "
> (JEREMIAH 1:6–7)

By that response God was teaching Jeremiah two things:

1. Do not think of yourself as inferior because you are young (or for any other reason).
2. Do not dismiss childlikeness as unimportant. It is those who are childlike who inherit the kingdom of God.

Pause to ponder...
1. Are you holding back in life because of an inferiority mindset?
2. Have you dismissed your childlike qualities for the sake of conformity?
3. What do God's words to Jeremiah say to you?

CLOSED BUDS

Lilian, a friend who loves plants and wildlife tended my little potted rose. Under my care it looked like the whole plant was dying! But when she removed the dead blooms she found lots of new buds waiting to open.

For some of us, it's as if those closed buds are parts of our personality or gifting that have never been able to come into being. We may experience this as a constant sense of feeling lost or empty, that we've got nothing to contribute. We may feel an ongoing ache or loneliness inside even when surrounded by people we love. We may have a whole pile of "I can'ts" stopping us in our tracks whenever we think of things we'd like to try. My friend Ann said, "That's me! I feel crippled and strangled by all the 'I can'ts'. I just can't imagine the freedom of 'I can.'" I was shocked by this comment as Ann has a very bubbly, fun-loving personality and I would never have guessed that was how she really felt about herself. Many of us are like Ann. We successfully hide our heartache, the feeling that something is missing. It can seem as if there is no answer – the lack of affirmation we experienced, the trauma we went through, the heavy weight of responsibility we had to carry at too young an age ... We feel, it's happened now, it's too late to change anything.

Humanly we may be right, but we have a God who is so much bigger than our limited human understanding. If He created us in the beginning can He not restore life to parts of His creation that have been blighted? We only have to look in our gardens to see how God has written renewal and restoration into the whole of creation. A tree appears dead in winter, but come spring new buds are pushing through and soon it is adorned with glory. A seed is planted and disappears into the earth. It could be forgotten, but God has put life within it of such a nature that it cannot remain in the form of a buried seed, but develops roots and shoots, pushing down and forcing its way up to light, beauty and fruitfulness. A hedgehog's heart rate slows down in winter to the extent that if it were human it would die. It disappears from our sight for months on end, seemingly dead. But in

the warmth of spring it comes to life again more full of
energy than before.

God loves the whole of you. He delights to recreate and restore you.
There is a wonderful promise in Joel 2:25:

> *"I will repay you for the years the locusts have eaten."*

And in Romans 4:17, referring to Abraham's faith in God:

> *"... the God who gives life to the dead and calls things that are
> not as though they were."*

Even a casual glance through the Bible reveals God's
delight in bringing life and making the impossible happen.
Think of Ezekiel called by God to prophesy life over the
valley of dry bones (Ezekiel 37) and the many prophecies
telling of desert places bursting into bloom, fresh water
pouring onto dry land, barren women giving birth ... God
cannot do things by half measure. If He died to save you, He
died for the whole of you, not just a part. He died to
completely destroy all the works of the evil one including
every strategy of his to rob us of life.

Ponder and pray...

You may feel that you are one of the "things that are not",
but God wants you to release those "nots" into His hands
and trust Him to love and speak them into life. We may
not know why they are there, but He knows. Give Him
permission to come into that dead or aching place and give
you His gift of healing life.

OPENING THE TRAPDOOR

The other week I had the opportunity to help out at a
church's parent and toddler group. I'd been joking for a few

days that doing this was making me step out of my comfort zone as I'd had very little to do with young children and felt I didn't know how to relate. I'd hidden my inadequacy behind a façade of being extremely admiring of those who had the children "knack". If I could affirm and encourage them in their gifting it would take the spotlight away from my own lack of ability!

But now I wasn't going to be able to hide any more, I'd been roped in to help.

On the morning of the club I was surprised at how panicky I felt. It seemed crazy to be so uptight over something so simple. I wasn't even going to be taking any real responsibility. I would just be there, alongside the toddlers and their parents. Moreover, it had been me in the first place who had offered to help, as I thought it high time I broke free from this inferior attitude. So why was I so afraid?

My friend popped in before I left home and said to me, "Relax and just enjoy playing with them!"

Without thinking, I answered, "But I don't think I know how to play!"

Somehow, in making that impulsive response I knew I had hit on a very painful truth. I felt close to tears, but had no time then to analyse what I had just said. It was time to go to the club.

The two hours went quickly and outwardly everything was fine. It was true I was quite awkward, not just with the children, but with their parents too. But I knew that was understandable. I am not a parent myself, I had never met any of them before and I couldn't hear them! But some of the mums were happy to jot down their comments in my notebook and I did manage to get alongside some of the children too. So in many ways all was fine and I enjoyed watching the children at play.

But in my heart something deep was happening.

Many of the children were between eighteen months and four years old. An exciting age of discovery. At first they were very clingy, refusing to leave their parents' sides. Gradually they became aware of all the exciting possibilities around them and dared to start to explore. A kaleidoscope of curiosity, fascination, touching, tasting, smelling, rolling, jumping, squidging clay, hopping, holding hands, butting tricycles, kissing, crying, laughing, running away from mummy, wanting cuddles with mummy...

I sat with some three-year-olds and their parents at the clay table. There were so many exciting stencils and shapes to use. A mum demonstrated how to flatten a piece of clay into a stencil and then fold the lid down over it to make the shape. A little girl watched her intently, then took her own lump of clay and happily proceeded to bang and smash it on the stencil, on the table and on the floor! There was no pretty shape at the end but there was a delighted little girl thrilled with the feeling of power, doing with her clay whatever she wanted to do.

I enjoyed observing all this, but inwardly, the more I saw of the children's freedom, the more I felt a pain, a huge emptiness and sense of loss. Why, I did not know, it was just a very deep aching that I could not put a name to. At the end I helped put the toys away, got back home, went to do some work on the computer and then started to cry!

I cried for a long time. It was a strange experience as I did not really know what was making me so sad. I felt it was something to do with seeing the children's freedom to be curious, to not have to follow a set way of doing things; their need to know mum or dad were there, tempered by their need to be themselves and to play in their own way. My response to my friend earlier that day, "I don't know how to play", was tearing at me inside, as if a voice was crying out:

'I don't know how to play. I don't know how to be a child, how to be curious, to enjoy discovery, to be relaxed in being me, Tracy. I feel so

afraid, so lost and alone, so much as if something is missing that has never come into being. I feel so sure in the child part of me, that whatever I do it will be wrong. I will be told off and disapproved of."

"WHEN I BECAME A 'MAN' I PUT CHILDISH WAYS BEHIND ME"

It is easy to think now we are grown up, that our childhood is just a part of the distant past. Many of us cannot even remember much of those years and any memories we do have may be so painful we don't ever want to go there again! What is the point, we think, of raking up past things? I am no longer a child, history is history and now I need to live in the present and for the future.

As Christians we may quote Paul's words to the Corinthians:

"When I was a child, I talked like a child, I thought like a child, I reasoned like a child. When I became a man, I put childish ways behind me."

(1 CORINTHIANS 13:11)

That seems so clear. Yes, there is a time and a place for the childishness of childhood, but on reaching adulthood that time is past and, like Paul, we have to be mature and choose to put the things of childhood behind us.

But is that really what Paul means?

Yes, it is true that *childishness* is not a good adult trait! A thirty-year-old's temper tantrum can be frightening. It is stressful being in a relationship with a forty-five-year-old who withdraws in petulant sulks, or a sixty-year-old who always has to have the last word, or a twenty-eight-year-old who hoards everything and won't share, an attention seeking fifty-two-year-old, or a thirty-nine-year-old who refuses to take any responsibility...

These are typical traits of childhood shared by all children to varying degrees. In that verse Paul is describing the normal stages of development where as we mature into adulthood we leave these ego-centred qualities behind and become "other"-centred – truly adult.

But often we try to leave many other aspects of our childhood behind too. The hurtful memories, the feelings of being small, helpless, vulnerable or afraid; the experiences of failure or loss or shame. We don't want our adult lives clogged up with all this so we push it into an inner room and lock the door on it. And it works! It can seem as if those things are truly gone as we get absorbed in our personal method of "growing up", pushing for success, money or possessions, multiple relationships, academic achievements, obsessive behaviour … But it's as if there's a hole in our lives that we've covered with a thin layer of sticks and none of these things we try can fill that hole. Only Jesus can do it.

PUTTING OUT THE RUBBISH

Sometimes we treat our inner child like we do our rubbish collections! We empty our household bins, tie up our sacks, put out our crates and leave everything outside. We then get on with our lives in the unshakeable knowledge that, bar a dustman's strike, in a few hours our rubbish will be gone, never to be seen again.

Unfortunately, locking the door on our childhood memories doesn't work in quite the same way. Instead of our inner rubbish being carted away and safely disposed of, it all piles up. We may have locked the door on it, but a small room can only hold so much. Things begin to seep out and we may find ourselves using yet another room as a dumping ground. But however hard we try we can find ourselves suddenly coming face to face with things we thought were long gone.

This was what happened to me in the mums and toddlers group. Seeing the growing independence of the children and their curiosity and delight, opened the door to one of my locked rooms and to feelings of loss and fear that I hadn't even been aware of.

When the tears of deep grief surfaced I had a choice: would I just push this all down again or would I let God deal with it? I decided to pray and ask God to illuminate what was happening in my heart so that I could deal with it properly. It's not enough to know that we have strong feelings. Both our hearts and our memories can deceive us. After all, when we suffer childhood hurts the very fact that we were children means that we didn't necessarily know the full picture or understand what was really happening.

BELIEVING A LIE

My father died of cancer when I was seven and for years I felt guilty. I believed that I was bad and somehow it was my fault he was gone. There was a particular memory that "proved" it to me. During the last weeks of his illness he was at home in a bed in the lounge. One night when I tried to wriggle close to him I was told to go up to bed, even though it wasn't yet my bedtime. I felt upset because everyone seemed tense and strange. My sister stayed down longer which made me feel excluded. I didn't know why I'd been sent up early. I couldn't sleep and when my sister eventually came up I was still awake. I could hear her crying and felt sick and afraid. Everything seemed different, but I didn't know why. When I went down the next morning my uncle was there and he and my nan and mum were all crying. Mum said through her tears, "Daddy's gone to heaven" but I only heard that he had gone. I'd never personally experienced death before and probably with my deafness had missed things in conversations and stories that help children learn about dying. All I knew was that I'd been sent to bed early which I associated with punishment, everyone was sad and Daddy had gone. I must have been so bad that I sent him away!

For years, well into my adulthood this guilt to do with my dad's death lay buried. Of course, I soon came to know he had actually died, not gone away, but my childish interpretation of the events of that night caused a lie of guilt to take root. Over the years this lie became toxic as I began to take responsibility for all the other bad things, believing somehow that, "I am to blame because I am the 'bad' one." I needed Jesus to shine His light of grace and truth into that web of lies and the character traits that had sprung out of it. Wonderfully, He did that. As I was receiving prayer on one occasion in my thirties, I "became" that frightened, guilty little girl alone in her room again. But suddenly He was there holding me close. I could feel His love and knew He wanted me to give to Him that heavy lie that I was bad. I was able to because I felt safe, as if I knew He knew everything. Then I could see myself in His arms being carried down to the lounge. We stood in the doorway together looking in and I "saw" my dad so ill in the bed and my mum trying to help him and my sister there too. It was as if a light came on in my heart and I suddenly "knew" that I'd been sent upstairs that night, not because I'd been bad, but because they wanted to protect me from seeing dad's final suffering. Far from being a punishment it was care for a small child.

Later that day, after that prayer, I was able to grieve properly for the first time for my dad and finally let him go.

God is always at work to reveal the truth and to bring restoration and healing. Paul tells us,

"He will bring to light what is hidden in darkness and will expose the motives of men's hearts."

(1 CORINTHIANS 4:5)

"The Spirit helps us in our weakness. We do not know what we ought to pray for, but the Spirit himself intercedes for us with groans that words cannot express. And he who searches our hearts knows the mind of the Spirit."

(ROMANS 8:26–27)

We often interpret that solely in terms of Spirit-led intercession for others, but we forget that Jesus is always interceding for us *all* and that applies to *me* as well as to the needs of the whole world!

DISCERNING THE SECRET PAINS

Now, on this present occasion with the stirred up grief from watching the toddlers, I needed to let Jesus in and shine His light into where these "groans that words cannot express" were coming from. I prayed He would protect me from all the lies of the enemy and lead me in such a way that I could grow into wholeness in this area of my life. I then sat quietly in His presence. Little "snapshots" began to come to mind: me in my toddler years seriously ill with encephalitis and in hospital. The "monsters" around me – I was in a ward for adult polio victims; they had big iron lungs over them. The sound of these was terrifying and I didn't know why I was there, why the nurses were so cross with me, why my body was acting so strangely. Associated feelings of fear and confusion came very strongly. I saw myself a little later, groping in the confusion that sound and vision were becoming, feeling alone and restricted.

The feeling that came to me was that of a very anxious little girl as if that vital part of my growth from babyhood into independence had never happened and was still trapped somewhere within me. I saw myself watching others to make sure I did things right, while at the same time knowing that I would inevitably do things wrong, desperately trying to get approval...

HEALING IS WORKING IN PARTNERSHIP WITH THE LORD

This poem, *I Remember When*, is a searching illustration of the need for true healing. The adult is happily talking to his inner child. He remembers only what he perceives as the good things of the past and is obviously in denial about what truly happened. He has chosen to rationalise it all, but in doing so has buried his hurts and emotions. The child is still there, however, trapped under the weight of all the rationalising. He needs a voice but isn't being given one. The only way he can become free is when the adult "notices" him and realises that his way is not the way of healing. Only him working together with Jesus can bring release from the past.

I Remember When
I remember when you could buy an orange with a
  tanner
And still have change for fish and chips and a day trip
  to the zoo,
Put a deposit on a bungalow, take the family out to
  see a show,
Ah! Those were the days; do you remember too?

And I remember when, Summer days were sunny,
When the sun shone strong and long from morn' till eve
And everyone knew wrong from right, school days were
  a pure delight,
Ah! Those were the days; it's hard now to believe.

But I remember when there wasn't any money,
And Mum went cleaning other people's floors

*And Dad was always down the pub; while he drank Mum would
   scrub,*
Then the bailiffs came knocking at the doors.

And I remember when school was really scary,
When the bullies seemed to pick me every time.
*And when we went on holiday, Mum and Dad would argue all
   the way,*
And somehow, I thought the fault was mine.

Ah! Yes, but I'm older now, and wiser with the
   passing of the years.
I understand my parents now,
I know more the "why", more the "how",
They were but the product of their childhood fears.

You see, I have learned to analyse, to justify and
   rationalise,
To see things from, well, an adult's point of view.
I've found ways to steer a path through life, avoiding
   unnecessary strife,
And, it's worked for me; it might work for you.

*Well, I'm really pleased for you up there, head in the clouds,
   nose in the air.*
I'm really glad you've found a way to cope.
*And whilst not wishing to complain, the truth is, I still feel the
   pain,*
And you are my only way of hope.

*So, will you please bring Jesus in, don't send Him but you
   come with Him,*
And introduce Him to the child inside.
*And let Him love away those fears and gather up those fallen
   tears,*
And bring to life the parts of us that died.

*Then, who knows, that faithful crutch, that you've relied upon
    so much,*
May now be placed upon God's Holy Fire.
*Where through those redeeming flames, you witness God's divine
    exchange,*
As He, in love, gives you your heart's desire.[4]

LETTING JESUS IN

A primary key to healing is realising that Jesus is not bound by time as we are. Hurts and fears, rage and control issues may have their roots in childhood traumas, but Jesus sees those traumas as if they are happening now and can transform them as we let Him into the memories. As that poem expressed, He will not heal and change us by force. He needs our partnership in the process. That partnership may lie in the simple act of asking for prayer and being willing to admit that we can't change ourselves, we need help.

We may need to forgive, both as adults and as the hurting child. Sometimes we need to consciously let our "little me" be loved by the present "adult me". Quite recently God spoke in my heart about me never having wanted to live and asked me to choose to be born again, not in the sense of being converted, but in the sense of coming into life welcomed by my Heavenly Daddy. It took much soul searching and agonising. I had to renounce the enemy's lying strongholds and accept that I was born by God's design. When I ultimately prayed, accepting myself as a tiny baby, birthed, held and wanted by my loving Heavenly Father, a tremendous peace washed over me and I had a desire to live my life "to the full" with Jesus. Interestingly, from that time on, my deep aversion to my name that I shared in Chapter 1 was healed and since then I have been fond of Tracy!

In this present pain of my toddler years I opened up to my friends Gill and Cathie and asked them to pray with me. Praying for the Holy Spirit's healing and release included playing as Gill brought out a basket of wooden blocks and we all built funny towers and shot a catapult at each other! I went from stiff self-consciousness to glee as I triumphantly smashed my tower down and "shot" Cathie! Later Cathie led me to recognise the many desires and dreams I had locked away with the key called "can't". I told Jesus I was sorry for hoarding "can'ts" when He'd already broken their power on the cross. I released them to Him and in faith received the treasures of: *"I can do everything through him who gives me strength"* (Philippians 4:13).

I am still working through these issues but know from within that Jesus is freeing and restoring me. Marilyn quoted someone the other day who said that "the atmosphere of the kingdom of heaven is restoration". A most beautiful thought. Where the spirit of God is, there is freedom, because He is love and He cannot help but bring restoration. All He asks is that we work in partnership with Him to bring that restoration about, both in our own lives and through us to others.

THE LOCKED CELLAR

In a concert I shared this picture from the Lord. I wrote it down afterwards and I share it here again now because I believe the Lord wants to touch some of you through it and bring healing.

> I saw a very smart house, every room decorated to a high standard. It was beautiful and looked flawless. Then the scene changed and I saw there was a locked cellar door. The Lord was standing at this door with you. He wanted your permission to open it and go

with you down the stairway into the dark cellar. But you were holding back, you wanted to run away and stay in the brightly ordered house. The Lord turned to you and said, "If a young child or even an animal were to fall into a hole and be helplessly stuck, wouldn't you do everything you could to get it out?"

Even as you thought, "Of course I would!" He looked at you and said, "You are that child. The 'adult you' has forgotten that you buried your 'child you' in this hole a long time ago, but now it is time to rescue and welcome that little one."

I then saw the two of you descending into the cellar. It is dark and cold but Jesus holds your hand and goes ahead of you and wherever He goes a pure, glowing light shines from Him. There are many things there piled higgledy-piggledy. Some you recognise, and with the recognition come strange overwhelming feelings. You grip Jesus' hand, dreading what is to come, yet strangely not wanting to let go or run away. He leads you to what looks like a child-sized bed and kneeling on the floor reaches under it and pulls out an old box. You feel terrified and hide behind Him as He opens the box to reveal a small child's soft toys. He reaches beneath the top ones and pulls out a cloth rabbit. Its ears are torn and hanging, an eye has been ripped out and it has lost its tail. You are weeping. You remember Rabbit. You would never go to bed without him! You weep as you remember your happy expectations. You would sleep safely with Rabbit. You would wake to a sunny day. You would be loved and have fun.

Grieving, you see that night you chose to bury Rabbit. When you shut the lid on him forever and "grew up". How terribly you missed him, but you shut the lid on that too. But now, as Jesus turns to you, cradling Rabbit in His arms, you suddenly know that the night you buried Rabbit you also buried yourself. You had not grown up. You were a little child, inseparable from your favourite toy and, with deep pain, you realise that from the moment you buried Rabbit you never expected it to be sunny again.

In the picture I see Jesus tenderly embracing you as you weep and indeed weeping with you. Then He holds Rabbit out for you to take: *"Be reconciled,"* He says, *"For I am the One who 'binds up the broken hearted; frees the captives from dark places and comforts those who mourn, replacing the ashes of their lost hopes and dreams with beauty and joy' "* (Isaiah 61:1–4 précis).

As I shared this in the concert it was as if a covering was removed from people's hearts. I looked over the sea of faces and many were in tears, struggling to contain their emotions. Marilyn and I prayed for several at the end. One person said that the rabbit was his. He'd completely forgotten it, but as I described the picture is was as if he was taken back and he remembered not only his rabbit but the traumatic event that had made him bury it. He cried as he shared with us and said that even though he was now in his forties he'd never been able to marry because he didn't know who he was, as if part of him was always missing. We prayed with him (and the other people) that he would be able to welcome both the rabbit (and all that symbolised of his lost innocence and joy) and his own little one back into his life and receive the Lord's healing and release. As he left us he was obviously feeling vulnerable and shaky, but his eyes, which had looked dark and empty when he first came up, now had a beautiful glow.

Obviously not everyone who asked for prayer had buried a literal toy rabbit! That was a symbol as much as a real event. It was all about the fact that we do lock things away and Jesus wants to enter into those memories and release us.

REFLECTION

- Find a place where you can be alone and quiet with the Lord. Have your journal to hand.
- Ask the Holy Spirit to protect you from the enemy's lies, to guide all your thoughts and enable you to hear His voice
- Prayerfully read that prophetic picture again. Does the image of going down into the cellar and finding the box of toys trigger any emotion or memory in you? If so write it down then ask the Lord to give you understanding and illumination about it.
- See Jesus turning to you with "Rabbit" in His arms. What is your "Rabbit"?
- Be real with Him, allow yourself to be and to feel. Can you sense His response? What is He doing?
- Does Jesus say anything to you or ask you to do anything? Ask Him for His power to do it. For example, to forgive someone or yourself, accept yourself, renounce a choice you made.
- In the light of this encounter with Jesus, reflect with thanksgiving on these incredible verses from Psalm 103, noting where I have added emphasis:

> *"Praise the LORD, O my soul,*
> *all my **inmost being**, praise his holy name.*
> *Praise the LORD, O my soul,*
> *and forget not all his benefits —*
> *who forgives **all** your sins*
> *and heals **all** your diseases,*
> ***who redeems your life from the pit***
> *and crowns you with love and compassion,*
> ***who satisfies your desires with good things***
> ***so that your youth is renewed like the eagle's."***
>
> (PSALM 103:1–5)

Notes

1. *My First Love*, © Stuart Townend.
2. *Live for a Change*, Francis Dewar (Darton, Longman & Todd, 1988 and 1999).
3. *The Logical Song* by Supertramp.
4. "I Remember When" from *Where is God? A Selection of Poems* by John Mockett, © 2005.

flying free
with God
living in the truth of God's healing love

CHAPTER 4

LEARNING
TO PLAY

"There is deep within all of us a voice. It speaks
to us continuously, knocking on the door of our
consciousness. When we are children the voice is very
loud ... [it] is the voice of wonder and amazement,
the voice of God which has always been speaking
to us, even before we were born."[1]

INFECTIOUS JOY

I love watching our animals play.

Pennie is a very quiet dog. She loves to sleep and most of
the time, when she isn't working with Marilyn, she is curled
up in a warm ball in front of the fire. But she has moments
when she seems to explode with joy. Just the other day I

took her to the field and let her off the lead. She stood still, head up to the sky, alert, poised as if listening for some signal. Then in a frenzy of excitement she took off, tearing round and round in ever increasing circles. Her joy was infectious, a wonderful picture of abandonment.

My friend Chris's granddaughter, Hazel, was born profoundly disabled mentally and physically. Yet despite being unable to do the things children take for granted, Hazel has an incredible gift of impacting those around her with joy. Her delight in simple things that catch her eye reaches into the place where most of us have forgotten to see from, the home of wonder, amazement, even exaltation. Chris says, for example, that when Hazel spies some sparkly wrapping paper, "Her facial expression and her fingers all spark like the paper. She is gasping with delight … her whole body becomes enthralled … you can just 'feel' her delight and you taste Heaven…"

Marilyn's previous guide dog, Giles,[2] delighted in play. He would pick up a pair of Marilyn's tights and would stand just out of reach with his ears pricked and tail wagging. A defiant stance, daring us to even try to retrieve the object! The moment we made the slightest move towards him he'd be off, charging down the lounge and up again through the kitchen with us in hysterical pursuit. It became such a favourite game that we would say, "Giles is going into chase" and everyone knew what we meant. He enjoyed "chase" to the full and, of course, we did too because as with Pennie and Hazel, joy is infectious.

ANIMALS AND CHILDREN – OUR TEACHERS

Animals, like children, teach us the true things of life. I love seeing little children at the seaside. Their amazement as they stand at the very edge firmly grasping daddy's hand; their patent disbelief that wherever they look there is water and yet more water! First tentative steps, cold, shock, laughter, tears, shrieks, splashing, paddling, running, dancing, buckets, moats, games – a whirlpool of fun and delight.

Maybe it was this ability to take delight in, to be amazed at, to throw ourselves into, to enjoy to the full, that made Jesus point to children as being the greatest in the Kingdom of Heaven.

> *"He called a little child and had him stand among them. And he said, 'I tell you the truth, unless you change and become like little children, you will never enter the kingdom of heaven. Therefore, whoever humbles himself like this child is the greatest in the kingdom of heaven.'"*
>
> (MATTHEW 18:2–4)

WHAT DOES IT MEAN TO BE LIKE A LITTLE CHILD?

What is Jesus talking about? What is He looking for in us? Our ability to experience the Kingdom of Heaven depends on this! How tragic if we missed it because we didn't think childlikeness an important enough issue! Jesus is not talking solely about how we become Christians, but about how we *live* as Christians. In fact, sadly, it is often *after* becoming Christians that we get bound up by rules and doctrines, committees and responsibilities that are all very serious and important, but somehow leave the adventure of trusting in God on the threshold of our lives. Jesus had the most important and serious mission there could ever be in the history of the world and therefore carried the greatest weight of responsibility, yet He shone with joy in His Father, love for people and delight in creation and all the different strands in everyday life through which God could be seen.

When my friend's daughter had her first baby recently I asked how she was getting on. My friend replied, "She's constantly worrying about everything and agonising over whether she is doing things right. I wish she'd just relax and enjoy her beautiful baby before too much time has rushed by."

The need to "do things right" became the sole motivation of the Pharisees and who could have been more joyless than them? This humorous yet telling little illustration shows how some of us interpret our Christian faith in an equally unsmiling way:

> "A little girl was out walking with her parents who belonged to a very strict sect of professing Christians ... A donkey put its head over a gate and she ran to pat it. She exclaimed, 'Oh Mummy, look! It must be a Christian donkey, it has such a long face!' "[3]

I used the word "unsmiling" deliberately because for many such Christians the issue is not that they don't love the Lord. Conversely, they love Him very much and are full of gratitude for what He did for them on the cross. That makes them very serious about how much they owe Him and they desire to serve Him and obey Him completely, yet somehow they miss the joy of relationship with Him, the very thing He died for. It is what I call the "Martha" mindset.

The Martha Mindset

"A woman named Martha opened her home to him. She had a sister called Mary, who sat at the Lord's feet listening to what he said. But Martha was distracted by all the preparations that had to be made. She came to him and asked, 'Lord, don't you care that my sister has left me to do the work by myself? Tell her to help me!'

'Martha, Martha', the Lord answered, 'you are worried and upset about many things, but only one thing is needed. Mary has chosen what is better, and it will not be taken away from her.' "

(LUKE 10:38–42)

DISTRACTED

There was no doubt that Martha loved the Lord and wanted to do her utmost for Him, but in the process she became distracted. This isn't a story about whether we should be busy or not, but about what is filling our hearts which the Bible refers to as the *wellspring of life*.

Distraction always has two sides to it.

1. *We get* distracted by . . .

Things jostle our minds or pull our hearts in all directions: people's demands or needs, the TV, Internet, phone or emails, our children, spouses or friends. Sometimes it's more insidious – our struggles, fears and inadequacies. Often, like Martha, the distracting element is the sense of what is expected of us and the resulting need to fulfil that or the fear that we won't fulfil it well enough. Francis Dewar gives this illustration:

> "We call this inner watchdog 'the parrot on my shoulder.' Many of us have an inner tyrant, critic or judge sitting like a parrot on our shoulder. For some, an inner school teacher is always telling you 'This is the proper way to do it.' Or an inner accuser is quick to point out, 'You made a right mess of that!' For others the inner parrot will say flatly, 'You can't do that, you're not clever enough.' . . . Start taking the parrot talk less seriously. Tell it to clear off . . . and be more open to your hidden depths and to the whisperings and nudgings of God."[4]

Mary made the better choice because she was "open to her hidden depths and the whisperings and nudgings of God" became more important to her than the pull of cultural expectations.

2. *We get* distracted from...

The different voices would be no problem if there wasn't something much better that they are pulling us away *from*. The disciples, like Martha, often failed to hear what Jesus was telling them because their thoughts and reactions were all over the place. The key difference with Mary was that she made a choice to give Jesus her entire attention. She wanted to look at Him while He was talking, to see His face and the expression in His eyes. She wanted to properly take in His words and not be half-listening as she clattered around in the kitchen!

I can identify with that because if I am going to hear someone at all I need to give them my full attention. Sometimes, because of time constraints, Marilyn tries to tell me things as she is moving around the kitchen opening cupboards, bending down, getting food out, etc. I, in the meantime, am chasing after her trying to get my ear in the right position to catch a sound! I often think we must look like Laurel and Hardy! But to have a proper conversation we sit together on the settee – where we can both give each other our full attention.

THE COST OF WORRY

Jesus said to Martha, *"You are worried and upset about many things..."* Worry fuels worry! Jesus knew by Holy Spirit revelation that for Martha the issue wasn't solely that she needed help in the kitchen. That was the straw that broke the camel's back, but there were many things fighting for space in her heart. It was as if her eye was reading an inner list of "I need to's" which stopped her from seeing Jesus and the opportunity that was before her to, *"Be still, and know that I am God"* (Psalm 46:10). Worry and anxiety are some of the traits of adulthood that Jesus wants us to lay down in order to become trusting and carefree like little children. The commands, "Do not worry" and "Do not fear" are some of the most numerous in the Bible! Why is this? Because the Kingdom of God is about bold faith and peace-filled trust in a God who is so much bigger than anything life can throw at us.

Pause to ponder...

- Martha was distracted *from* Jesus *by* the pull of anxiety and cultural expectations.
- Mary was distracted *from* cultural expectations *by* the lure of being with Jesus.

THE LURE
OF BEING WITH JESUS

Reflect

- What kind of distractions pull you away from being with Jesus?
- What kind of choices might you need to make to become like Mary?
- We cannot literally sit at His feet and listen to His voice, yet He is with us just as much as He was with Mary. All of us have different things that draw us into His presence. Do you know yours? Tick any of these examples that are "you"? Add others in the blank spaces.

Reading and studying the Bible, and being taught by inspired Bible teachers. Hearing God's voice through His Word, obeying His Word.	*"I rejoice in following your statutes ... I meditate on your precepts ... I delight in your decrees"* (Psalm 119:14–16).

Worship and praise with others or alone, singing, making music, dancing, voice and body praise, song writing.	*"Praise God in his sanctuary; praise him in his mighty heavens. Praise him for his acts of power"* (Psalm 150:1–2).
The beauty of creation, seeing and being in it, gardening, farming, working with plants, animals, babies, walking, photography, art, poetry, drama . . .	*"When I consider your heavens, the work of your fingers . . . O LORD, our Lord, how majestic is your name in all the earth!"* (Psalm 8:3, 9)
Silent prayer and contemplation, Holy Communion, using symbols like candles, banners, the cross, meditation, conversing with God.	*"My heart says of you, 'Seek his face!' Your face, LORD, I will seek"* (Psalm 27:8).
Serving others, caring for those in need, giving to the poor, praying for the sick, reaching out to the lonely, showing mercy.	*"I tell you the truth, whatever you did for one of the least of these brothers of mine, you did for me"* (Matthew 25:40).
Stepping out in the power and resources of the Holy Spirit to do the works of Jesus, ministering, prophesying, evangelising, healing . . .	*"Follow the way of love and eagerly desire spiritual gifts, especially the gift of prophecy"* (1 Corinthians 14:1).

- Spend a few moments now to draw close to Him and chat with Him about your responses.
- Ask Him to help you discover Him in some of the ways you are not so familiar with.

BECOMING LIKE LITTLE CHILDREN

Children are born with a natural sense of trust and expectancy. They are spontaneous, open and joyful. They want to know "why" and they're not afraid to ask that over and over! They are curious and in that curiosity unfettered by what is or isn't appropriate or what is apparent to the eye and what is mystery. They want to discover, to learn and to be. They are courageous pioneers and survivors in a strange and sometimes hostile world. They need to push the boundaries of what they are "told" and test the water for themselves.

Sadly, nowadays, children are under such pressure to grow up quickly and to be seen as streetwise that they early lose their sense of innocent wonder and childlike enthusiasm. To be cynical and disdainful is cool in today's society for both young and old, but at what cost have we and our children renamed our childlike wonder, naivety and thrown it in the tip?

Some time ago I read this challenging piece entitled *Youth*. This is not referring to physical age so much as being about the way we can grow old in our hearts and spirits when we let go of the joy of life. We forget to practise thanksgiving and we sacrifice our God-given ideals to the worries of life.

"Youth is not a time of life, it is a state of mind. Nobody grows old merely by living a number of years; people grow old only by deserting their ideals. Worry, doubt, self-distrust, fear and despair; these are the long,

long years that bow the head and turn the growing spirit back to dust. You are as young as your faith, as old as your doubt, as young as your hope, as old as your despair. So long as your heart receives messages of beauty, cheer, courage, grandeur and power from the earth, from man, from the infinite, so long are you young. When the heart is covered with the snow of pessimism and the ice of cynicism, then I am grown old indeed, and may you, Lord, have mercy on my soul."[5]

This quotation made me think of an elderly lady, Miriam, who Marilyn and I once stayed with. She was bubbling over with enthusiasm, sharing all the Lord was doing in her life. She had so much energy as she bustled around bringing tea and delicious homemade biscuits. She told us that when she'd reached seventy she said to the Lord that she didn't want to get old! The Lord told her to spend each year learning something new. The first year she learnt to cook and enjoy Indian food. The next year she bought a computer. The following year she started learning to play an electric keyboard. All we could think to say was, "Wow!" What an amazing attitude to old age. I know that I would love to enter those years with as much enthusiasm! Here's another example of a childlike old lady:

"A little girl looked at a very old lady and said 'Are you very old?' After a pause the lady smiled and replied, 'No, I wouldn't say that I was old, but I must admit that I've been young for an awfully long time!'"[6]

Pause to ponder...
Reflecting on these thoughts and without going by your actual age in years, would you call yourself an "old" or a "young" person?

How can we become young again? Thankfulness is a key.

"My heart leaps for joy
and I will give thanks to him in song."

(PSALM 28:7)

Once I was waiting for a bus that showed no sign of coming. The buses have to be extremely close for me to see their numbers, so each time one comes I am full of hope, only to be disappointed at the last minute! Today was no exception. One bus had come and gone and the next was well over twenty minutes late. I was fed up and felt like giving someone a belting! When I eventually got home I had to empty the bin and spent several minutes trying to prise a black bin liner open. In my frustration I shook it so hard that it crackled loudly, terrifying the cat!

Suddenly a thought dropped into my mind:

"What a grumpy old bag you are! Where's your thankfulness?"

I was shocked, the bin liner hanging limply from my hand. It hadn't even occurred to me to be thankful that irritating day!

"There's no one around so why bother!" was my muttered reaction.

Have you ever realised God speaks through His silence?

This was a real silence as if a CD had suddenly been turned off. No thoughts dropping into my mind, no pictures or verses, just the silence of His presence. And I knew it was His hurt presence. I had just called Him "nobody" and dismissed all reasons for thanking Him; yet there were many reasons, many ways in which He'd shown His love for me that day.

"Lord, I am so sorry," I said.

I knew that He still loved me, but longed for me to have a wider vision. How could I have been so miserable about silly things like buses and bin bags when *He* was at my side all the time? There are so many beautiful things all around me He wants to draw my attention to, if only I had eyes to see. He wants the joy of intimacy and sharing precious moments together.

"Lord, please give me that wider vision," I prayed. *"I am sorry for being a moaner and being sucked into the 'fed up' ethos of our culture. Help me to become your joy catcher and spreader."*

Later, I stood at the bus stop again and the bus was late! Tension was rising but I suddenly remembered my prayer. I silently welcomed Him at my side and asked Him to give me childlike eyes to see His joy. My eye was drawn to a boy of about nine walking with his mum. He was holding her hand and skipping. I felt Jesus' great pleasure in his happy close-ness to his mum, in his freedom to enjoy childlike pleasures.

A very old lady, bent double with arthritis struggled to get off a bus, a line of people waiting behind her, including a teenaged boy. He pushed towards the old lady and I tensed thinking he was going to shove her aside. But he offered her his arm and helped her down. I sensed the Lord had tears in His eyes as He rejoiced in this youth's kindness. My own eyes filled and I realised how present the Lord is in all that happens around us. He longs for us to see with His eyes of love and respond from His heart of joy.

Later I read this extract from a talk by Mother Teresa which challenged me even more:

"Those who are materially poor can be very wonderful people. One evening we went out and we picked up four people from the street. And one of them was in a most terrible condition. So I did for her all that my love can do. I put her in bed, and there was such a beautiful smile on her face. She took hold of my hand as she said one word only: 'Thank-you' – and she died. I could not help but examine my conscience. And I asked, 'What would I say if I were in her place?' And my answer was very simple. I would have tried to draw a little attention to myself. I would have said, 'I am hungry, I am dying, I am cold, I am in pain.' But she gave me much more – she gave me her grateful love. And she died with a smile on her face.

Then there was the man we picked up from the drain, half eaten by worms and, after we had brought him to the home, he only said, 'I have lived like an animal in the street, but I am going to die as an angel, loved and cared for.' After we had removed all the worms from his body, all he said, with a big smile, was, 'Sister, I am going home to God' and he died. It was so wonderful to see the greatness of that man who could speak like that without blaming anybody, without comparing anything. Like an angel – this is the greatness of people who are spiritually rich even when they are materially poor."[7]

Pause to ponder...

- Have you thanked the Lord for anything today?
- Have you taken the time and thought to thank someone who has offered you a kindness?
- Pray Jesus gives you eyes to see the ordinary things of life through His eyes of joy.

ENJOYING THE PRESENT MOMENT

One thing I have often noticed about young children is their ability to live in the present moment. A favourite film, a computer game, a tower they are building, a puddle they are stomping in ... every bit of their attention is focused on that one thing. The moment may be very brief and all too soon they want to do something else, but the key is, they have actually lived in and experienced *that moment*. As adults we often hold many things in our minds at the same moment, usually in the form of tasks we need to accomplish or goals we need to meet. This makes us great achievers, but can also create a deep sense of dissatisfaction. It means we are often blind to the things that bring the greatest joy. I was very challenged recently by the following poem published on the Internet. It was written by a teenage girl dying of cancer who was desperate to help people see life differently, to stop and really look:

"Have you ever watched kids on a merry-go-round?
Or listened to the rain slapping on the ground?
Ever followed a butterfly's erratic flight?
Or gazed at the sun into the fading night?
You better slow down, don't dance so fast,
Time is short, the music won't last.

Do you run through each day on the fly?
When you ask, 'How are you?'
Do you hear the reply?
When the day is done, do you lie in your bed,
With the next hundred chores
Running through your head?
You'd better slow down, don't dance so fast
Time is short, the music won't last.

Ever told your child, 'We'll do it tomorrow'
And in your haste not seen his sorrow?
Ever lost touch, let a good friendship die?
'Cos you never had time to call and say 'Hi'?
You'd better slow down, don't dance so fast
Time is short, the music won't last.

When you run so fast to get somewhere
You miss half the fun of getting there

When you worry and hurry through your day
It is like an unopened gift thrown away.
Life is not a race, do take it slower,
Hear the music before the song is over."[8]

NOTICING GOD

When I was first a Christian I attended a Christian Fellowship. Deliverance and healing were key themes and every member knew that God could do mighty things through them. The worship was exuberant with expressive lyrics.

All of this was a dynamic mix and I personally experienced much healing through this church and was released into my prophetic gifting. But one thing I seemed to lack was a sense of the character of God. What was He actually like, this God who was so powerful? As a deaf person a person's body language is always important and helps me to discover their giftings, loves and hates. But although I knew that Jesus healed and delivered people and showed us God's love through everything He said and did, I couldn't *see* what He was actually like!

This began to change at a deep level when I went to a retreat centre in 2004. Each day I would share my day's experiences with my retreat leader, Mags, or we'd think about a Bible verse together. She would often ask me something like, *"Who is the God you met in that experience ... or in this Bible passage?"*

At first I was stunned wondering what on earth she meant! Then I realised she was opening up a path of discovery into God's character and the many ways He comes to us. To notice not just that He has done certain things or spoken to people to challenge or comfort them, but also *in what way* He was doing that. This kind of *noticing* is much more than a casual glance at what a passage is about. It is more like a Holy Spirit inspired reflection and conversation with God enabling us to see in a new way who God is and what He is like.

So, for example, I was very familiar with the awesome stories of Jesus miraculously feeding thousands of people, but I'd never had any sense of His *manner* as He did these miracles. I will never forget my wonder when I asked Him for revelation so that I could *notice Him* in that story. Suddenly it was as if I was there as a hidden observer, as if Jesus and I were in it together. I saw Jesus' delight in the plan that was bubbling inside Him, even through all the hours and days of teaching and healing the crowds. As if He was saying to His Father, *"They think they've seen it all with these miracles, but the icing on the cake is still to come! How I love to surprise them and show them there is always more!"*

I saw His love for His bewildered disciples as they flapped around in exasperated confusion. He was there as Friend and Mentor as well as miracle worker. I sensed His wisdom in making His disciples share in the outworking of His plan so that it would be their experience as well as their observation. I saw the disbelieving crowd, certain He was crazy yet still longing for something beyond the impossible. And as He prayed and blessed the paltry number of fish and loaves, I saw how He was inwardly chuckling with His Father knowing what was about to unfold. Through all this I realised that Jesus was *playing* His miracle! He was full of joy and delight, laughing at the disciples perplexed astonishment as loaves and fish multiplied in their own hands.

GOD IS EXCITING, ZANY AND FULL OF ADVENTURE

Why did God appear to Moses in a bush? Why did He use the bizarre experience of being eaten alive by a whale to get through to His delinquent prophet? Why did He make Abraham count stars and Gideon count men who lapped like dogs? Why did He devise strange battle strategies for the army of God such as marching seven times around a city then all shouting together? Just imagine if our army did that in Afghanistan! Why did He anoint a judge's long hair with divine strength? Why did He ask Hosea to marry a prostitute and Ezekiel to lie on his left side for over a year? What was in God's mind when He caused frogs and locusts to overrun Egypt and when He split the waters of the Red Sea in two? What did He feel as He created each mountain range, each waterfall, each galaxy and form of life? What was in His heart as He cradled newly created man in His hands and then gave him divine authority to bestow identity and purpose on each animal? What incredible trust! Why did He cause His only Son to be born in a stable? What compelled Him to have that same Son murdered on a cross and then to burst through the prisons of death with Resurrection power?

Seeing these examples of God's astonishing actions and ways grouped together like this, and knowing there are countless more than I have described, fills me with exhilaration. We truly have an amazing God. He is unseen yet loves to be sought and found. He is beyond our imagining, yet loves to make Himself known. He loves to astound and to melt away our rigid mindsets. With a word He spoke this universe into being and with another word He yields that same authority to us.

As I prayerfully reflect a thought comes overwhelmingly: *To play is God's work and God's delight.*

For us to be like little children is to have hearts to play as God plays. A child's playfulness becomes the foundation of a believer's prayerfulness.

A STORY OF A PLAY/PRAYER EXPERIENCE

The following account is lifted directly from my journal when I was at the retreat centre in 2004. God had been touching some deep issues in my life and I'd shed many tears as I faced shame and fear from the past and experienced the Lord's tender compassion. Now I was about to discover a different Jesus!

"Walked outside a different way. Came to an incredible tree with its branches kneeling on the ground. Is it worshipping? Leant against them. It is a beautiful, peaceful spot with trees kind of dancing together. Chat to Jesus again.

'Can you use me, Lord? How can I love people like you do?'

At that point the sunshine broke out through the leaves and I felt its warmth on me and sensed Jesus was replying:

'I want to grace people with My love; to reach into the cold places in their hearts and warm them with the fire of My love that never goes out. I want to tell them I love them, that I know everything and still love them. I long to draw them up into Myself, to help them see I carry their pain and want to give them something precious.'

I am awed by this, realising I have heard His heart. I then suddenly have the feeling Jesus wants me to try to climb this tree! I must be mad. I ask Jesus if I am mad? I am forty! I've got bad balance. Suppose I get stuck or fall out, then what? Surely it's too frivolous to think of climbing a tree on a serious retreat!

'Child, I am the God of laughter as well as tears. You've wept with Me in the chapel now come and laugh and have fun with Me.'

I wriggle up and manage to crawl backwards up the branch after first having a loving embrace with a thorn bush! Sit between two branches feeling pleased, but really I am only about two or three feet up. Feel He wants me to go higher! 'Lord, this is crazy, suppose someone sees me?'

'*Who cares?*'

'Well, You'd better make sure I don't fall!'

Twist round and manage to stand on lower branch while holding on higher. Easy! Climb higher, all except my right arm which is nicely hooked around another thorny twig. Try to swing it free and nearly fall off! Almost swear, then remember Jesus is with me! Begin to giggle as I think of me and Jesus being stuck in a tree together. Feel He is enjoying it with me. Amazing. Realise it's not the first time Jesus has been stuck on a tree and am quickly sobered. I embrace it and rest my head in it feeling the extreme roughness on my face. How it must have torn Him already being so wounded. Thank Him quietly then carry on climbing. Really, I would like to get to the place a few feet further up where the branch levels out and joins the trunk. If this is symbolising me stepping out with Jesus maybe I should, but I have already taken quite a few steps and I need to be sensible! I've still got to get down. Rest there for a bit. Very conscious of Jesus there with me. Only me and Him in this improbable place. No one else knows where we are! Lovely to worship from this new viewpoint as I can suddenly hear the wind in the leaves and the birds. I feel the buds near me, they are sticky. I never knew that before. In fact, I didn't know buds could be on trees at this time of year.

Time to get down. This is the difficult bit. Not sure how to turn around and once turned how to step back down branch. Can Jesus help me? Feel I should turn again and go backwards, but get stuck with one leg forward, one back. Start to laugh again as I imagine how I must look! I was telling Mags I wanted to be poised earlier! Soon giggling helplessly, hope no one on retreat comes by! Manage to get down in the end after another encounter with the thorn bush!"[9]

A Prayer Reflection

Spend a few minutes reading these words from Proverbs describing the relationship between Jesus and His Father as together they made this universe.

- Ask the Holy Spirit to help you *notice* God in new ways.
- What means the most to you in this passage?
- What expression can you "see" on Jesus' face as He works alongside His Father?
- If you use one word/phrase to describe their heart attitude to their work what would it be?
- Can you use the same word, or would you like to do so, about the things in your life?
- Tell Him your response and longings and spend time praising Him for His passionate love and joy in all He does.

"I was appointed from eternity,
  from the beginning, before the world began . . .
I was there when He set the heavens in place . . .
when he gave the sea its boundary . . .
and when he marked out the foundations of the earth.
  Then I was the craftsman at his side.
I was filled with delight day after day,
  rejoicing always in his presence,
rejoicing in his whole world
  and delighting in mankind."

(Proverbs 8:23, 27, 29–31 précis)

Message Through a Painting

The other day I was trying to paint a picture. It was a sudden impulse as I am no artist! Faced with the blank sheet of paper I didn't know what to do, but decided to fill it with colour and see what it turned into. As I applied the various hues it was as if my imagination took flight and I saw in it a beautiful seascape with the sun setting in the distance. Trees were added in the foreground and boats appeared, sailing across the golden path of the sun. People were walking along the edge of the shore looking out at the beauty. Birds flew in the sky and rugged cliffs took shape in the distance. All of this sounds as if I suddenly discovered a Van Gogh gifting! Not at all! Anyone who looked at my painting would have had trouble recognising what it was meant to be. To the casual eye it just looked like a glorious muddle of colours streaked over the page. Is it an abstract or what?

But in my heart as I painted and imagined and added colours and shapes to fulfil that imagining and fleshed it out, I began to sense God speaking to me:

"You have turned a blank piece of paper into something unique and beautiful. It has come alive under your touch. You have seen in your mind's eye what it was to be and have created that. This picture is part of you and has come from you. No other picture will be quite the same. It is a unique creation. In that same way I have formed you. I saw in My mind's eye all you were to be, a beautiful imagining from which I knew what colours and patterns to paint into your life. You are unique. You have an identity that has come from Me and has been written into your makeup. No one else can ever replicate that. As you open up to Me, the artist, who painted your life with such delight, you will see what that picture truly is. You will look and the mystery will become clear and you too will know that joy."

I was awestruck. There was suddenly such a powerful sense of the presence of God. But I had just been having a bit of fun painting in order to relax. I wasn't trying to be spiritual; in fact I'd felt a bit guilty for "wasting time" like this! God viewed it differently. He had used that simple "play" activity as a means of speaking to me and revealing His heart of joy in all His children and in all His works. As I wrote out these prophetic words from God I prayed that I would encounter Him more and more through the everyday things in my life and that as I learnt to "play" and to become like a little child, I would enter more fully into His kingdom and live in that place where a childlike playfulness would become the essence of powerful prayerfulness.

Maybe you'd like to receive this prophetic word from your Father God for yourself and let my prayer response inspire your own response.

Notes

1. *Dangerous Wonder* by Michael Yaconelli, © 1998, Navpress Books.
2. At time of writing, March 2008, Giles is fourteen and living with friends. He is arthritic so can't run as he did, but is as enthusiastic as ever, especially for stolen treats!
3. A true story from Ireland taken from *Out of the Mouths of Babes* collected by Phil Mason, © 1999.
4. *Live for a Change*, Francis Dewar.
5. © General Douglas Macarthur.
6. *Out of the Mouths of Babes*, Phil Mason.
7. Mother Teresa of Calcutta at the National Prayer Breakfast in Washington DC, 3 February 1994.
8. Posted on the internet 2006. Written by a teenager who was terminally ill with cancer and desperate for people to learn to treasure life before it is too late. She wanted the message to get out to as many people as possible before she died.
9. Taken directly from my journal written on my retreat at Loyola Hall, October 2004. I had my notebook in my pocket and wrote it as I sat on the level branch in the tree.

flying free
with God

living in the truth of God's healing love

CHAPTER 5

GOD WANTS INTIMACY WITH YOU

"Being the Beloved is the origin and the fulfilment of
the life of the Spirit."[1]

HAVE YOU ENCOUNTERED GOD'S LOVE FOR YOU?

God's love is reaching out to you and has been since the
beginning of time. His love is like the breaking light of dawn
or the rays of the rising sun piercing the darkness and
writing a golden pathway across the restless seas. His love is
the nudging in our spirits as we sleep; the call to wakefulness
and the opening of the adventure of a new day. His love

makes a pathway where there is only undergrowth. It creates a door where there is only a wall. It opens up a channel in our hearts through which pure streams can flow. It thaws and melts us inside our lives and releases us to love in a different way. From the heavens to our hearts His love emblazons the message, *"You are my Beloved One. On you My favour rests."*

Pause for thought

- Do I know myself as Beloved to God?
- Have I explored what God's love means to me and the pathways of my own desire for God?

PRETENDING WE DON'T HAVE WEAKNESSES

God calls us His beloved children and this is our true identity. But often life and the devil have convinced us that to be beloved we must be perfect and therefore weaknesses, both in ourselves and in others, are not acceptable. We can spend all our energy trying desperately to be something we are not when we live with this attitude.

We hear it preached that *"with God we shall gain the victory"* (Psalm 60:12). But we forget that words like "victory" are war words and war is about struggle and passion and belief in the rightness of who you are and what you are doing. You cannot have victory without engaging an enemy who is bent on defeating you. Every ounce of your resources has to be brought into play to defeat that enemy, but then comes the victory! To be honest, if that wasn't the case, victory to me would have a very hollow feel to it. True victory is nothing to do with jumping around happily in a charismatic worship style, although heartfelt worship and thanksgiving have a mighty place in bringing victory about. Once I said to my retreat leader when I was struggling with a lot of issues,

"I know I need to be praising Him a lot more..." She replied with the following:

> "I do not for one minute believe that God needs praise, so much as He needs you to notice that He is with you. The quiet sense of being in His presence is celebration enough for Him. He doesn't need our praise, He needs relationship. Praise and worship can be a very good way of keeping God at arm's length. Noticing Him in the midst of the chaos is real and intimate. I think the most challenging thing to process is the fact that God is comfortable with our brokenness – He doesn't need us to be undamaged, but in order to fully appreciate our identity, we need to integrate the brokenness and the blessing. We need to find a way to hold it all together, because in that effort grace seems to flow."

Pause to ponder...

Victory is not denying we have struggles and brokenness, but owning it as part of who we are while still choosing to open ourselves to "Immanuel, God with us" in the midst of it.

I told the Lord that I want to learn to truly be with Him and be real with Him as a friend, because He is with *me* in all things even when I am in the midst of upset. One of my ongoing "mountains" of struggle, self-pity and resentment is with my deafness. Speech sounds like a foreign language and as someone who loves people, I often feel very isolated. I have experienced the healing of the Lord in so many deep areas in my life and know His anointing as I step out in ministry situations. Yet in this area I often just stick a "Christian" smile on my face and hide my feelings as there seems no easy solution other than to grin and bear it!

So now I told Him I was sick of feeling disconnected and like a foreigner. I asked Him to help me to stop hiding behind my deafness because I really want to be someone that reaches out to people and draws them to Him.

After praying I felt very relaxed in the way you can feel when you spontaneously share with a trusted friend. Jesus is that friend to us, but sadly we don't always practise the reality of that friendship in the way Peter urges us:

> *"Cast all your anxiety on him because he cares for you."*
> (1 PETER 5:7)

I sensed Him gently encouraging me to look outward not inward any more and He would show me Himself and satisfy my desire to have more connection with people. My sense of struggle was still there, but I felt as if I was now looking towards Him with a new expectation that He would be alongside me, helping me.

Later, I needed to make things right with someone I'd let down. I had written her a grovelling email that morning, but not yet sent it. I was about to click on "send" when I felt an inner nudging to wait. I was surprised, but the feeling was very strong so I did wait. I was amazed when just a few minutes later a Live Messenger contact flashed up on my screen and I realised it was this very person! Her message was warm and showed no trace of upset. I was full of awe at how the Lord had stepped in just in time. How wonderful that He was involved in my emails to the extent that He knew when I was about to click my mouse! I knew, as if a light was suddenly turned on, that if I had sent that grovelling email it would have had a very detrimental effect indeed.

In town later at the building society, I was at the counter while the cashier dealt with my business. I often feel intimidated by people. Not usually because they are intimidating, but just because I can feel a fool with my deafness and I transfer it onto them. Suddenly this lady made a joke about trying to do several jobs at once and I was able to suss her comments and joke back. She then complimented me on my glasses. She wore glasses too, so again we were able to chat for a few moments in a normal way and it was as if the deafness didn't matter and I was connecting in a simple but lovely way with a normal person doing her job. I felt the Lord's loving presence with me. He was showing me that I just need to relax and He will give me more opportunities to connect with people in a natural way.

It may seem strange to make much of a brief encounter like that, but for me such times become precious moments as if I have come off an island where I am the sole inhabitant! I felt full of joy that the Lord was truly with me and showing me that the deafness need not be an impassable mountain. I am far more than a deaf person, far more than someone who has experienced a painful childhood. I may be a clay pot, but I have the treasure of God's Kingdom inside me and so do you!

LOVE AND BE LOVED

Today, in church my pastor showed us a large oil painting that he had been given when ministering in Argentina. At the end of the service I went up to look at it more closely. It was beautiful in its simplicity. A wooden boat at rest in still waters, its pure reflection broken only by the gentle ripples of the sea in the changing light. Beyond it, the expanse of sea and sky stretched away into the distance. To me it conveyed a sense of peace and yet also of challenge and adventure. What would happen when the boat sailed forward into the unknown? What new things were there for it to discover? I felt I wanted to board it and sail away into the light that surrounded it!

My pastor shared how drawn he had been to this picture and how, as he'd spent time gazing at it, he experienced a deep sense of joy and discovery. The picture was so simple and yet touched something very deep in his soul. As often as he looked at it, he could always find something new and fresh to see. To him it conveyed the paradox of the peace and safety of our relationship with God, run through with the challenge of new adventure, the pull of golden light on the horizon, the ripples of the shallows drawing us into the depths of God's love.

He likened it to the joy of looking for God and finding Him, of gazing through the window of all we know of God, yet always the possibility of discovering something new. David and other psalmists expressed this same joy and longing. They wanted to know God, to experience Him and meet with Him; to be able to see beyond human limitations to the truth of who God is and what He is like and to bask in that truth and be empowered from within to work out their purpose for living. We see their longing expressed over and over in the Psalms:

"One thing I ask of the LORD,
*   this is what I seek,*
that I may dwell in the house of the LORD
*   all the days of my life,*
to gaze upon the beauty of the LORD
*   and to seek him in his temple."*

(PSALM 27:4)

"My heart says of you, 'Seek his face!'
*   Your face, LORD, I will seek."*

(PSALM 27:8)

"My soul yearns, even faints
*   for the courts of the LORD;*
my heart and my flesh cry out
*   for the living God."*

(PSALM 84:2)

"As the deer pants for streams of water,
so my soul pants for you, O God.
My soul thirsts for God, for the living God.
Where can I go and meet with God?"

(PSALM 42:1–2)

AN IMPOSSIBLE DREAM?

Listening to my pastor and reading these verses, I felt sad. Sad because it seemed that to have such a longing as the psalmists expressed went beyond what was humanly possible to experience. I could not imagine wanting to live in church and spend all my time gazing at someone invisible! I wanted to know God, but I could hardly say that I was as consumed with desperation as a thirsty deer. I am not actually very familiar with the habits of deer, but I do have a fair bit of experience with thirsty dogs! I've watched Marilyn's guide dogs drink and drink as if they haven't seen any water for months on end and have no hope of getting more. An entire bowlful emptied in moments and then another. All this is in wet and rainy England, not even the dry desert that the psalmists were so familiar with. I knew that my passion for God's presence was nothing like that. Was I just very un-spiritual or was I missing something?

HIS LOVE IGNITES OURS

Later that afternoon I decided to pray about my coldness and lack of desire for the Lord. I felt anxious that I seemed to be so far away from Him, in comparison to the psalmists. I sat at my big desk and was trying hard to concentrate when suddenly there was a thump in front of me and a soft tapping on my hand. When I opened my eyes there was Zoë my cat! She gazed at me intently, stepped delicately onto my lap and started rubbing her head against me, purring so hard that her whole body vibrated with the sound.

"Oh, Zoë," I said, lifting her to the ground, "not now, I'm praying!" But Zoë would not be put off. She marched back and forth on my desk batting at me every time I tried to close my eyes. She pressed into my lap again, pushing her head under my chin. Then to my alarm, she jumped on my computer keyboard, writing her own paragraphs in the process! The more I tried to push her away the more she purred! I felt irritated that she was interrupting my time with God in such a rude way and yet I was actually enjoying her affection, even while exasperatedly pushing her away! Eventually she padded out of the room. Relief, I thought, now I can try to be spiritual. I closed my eyes and tried to pick up my prayer again, but felt a sudden nudging on my knee. Not again! This time Pennie, Marilyn's guide dog, was gazing at me imploringly. Even as I shook my head and said, **"Bed!"** she tapped me on my knee with her paw while frantically wagging her tail. I patted her head, fondled her ears, then tried to get back to prayer but to no avail. Pennie continued pawing and to add insult to injury, Zoë returned and leapt back onto my lap purring and nuzzling me!

Defeated, I looked at my watch, it was 6 pm. I was about to get up and do some jobs when everything seemed to take on an edge and significance as if a camera had zoomed into close up. I looked at Zoë still sitting on my desk, staring at me intently, and Pennie gazing up at me offering her paw. What was happening? Was God trying to make me aware of something? Did He want to speak to me? Strangely, the time also seemed significant so I looked at my watch again. It was now just after 6 pm.

"What are you saying to me, Lord? Why have I suddenly become so aware of Zoë and Pennie? They've just ruined my prayer time with You!"

And suddenly a light shone in my mind. I realised that

God *was* indeed speaking to me. He was pointing me to the fact that it was tea-time for the animals and they were trying to tell me! Marilyn and I always fed them in the in the early evening. That routine had created, in its turn, an expectation to be fed. This acted as a trigger, compelling and releasing them to be affectionate and loving towards us particularly when it approached tea-time! The ability to be affectionate and loving was in their make-up, but needed igniting by what they received from us.

God was speaking in answer to my prayer. All through my efforts to push the distracting animals away, He was gently trying to show me that they were part of His answer. Our care for the animals had ignited a loving response from them to us. Similarly, in our own lives, we can only love God, delight in Him and gaze upon His beauty as we first receive His love for us. This then ignites our ability to love Him in return!

With this revelation my heart opened up. I felt amazed how God had spoken to me through the pets and was comforted, realising that such a desire to see the Lord as the psalmists' expressed – to love Him and discover Him – could only have been fired by experiencing God's love for them. We cannot love in a void. As John tells us,

"We love because he first loved us."

(1 JOHN 4:19)

Pause for thought

- God spoke to me through my pets. In the same way Jesus heard His Father's voice as He watched the birds, flowers, children, farmers, housewives . . .
- Do you expect to hear God speaking to you through everyday things?
- Do you let the things you find your attention drawn to become doorways to a conversation with God?

DISCOVERING THAT GOD NOT JUST LOVES BUT LIKES YOU!

Today, God spoke again to me through Zoë.

Marilyn brought me an early morning cup of tea and as she opened the door, Zoë stalked in, gazed at me and then very deliberately jumped up on my bed and started nuzzling me. She was full of affection and although there were several places in the house where she loved to curl up to sleep, it seemed that she just wanted to be with me!

I was pleased to see her and to feel her contented purrs. It made all the difference to waking up. But as I sat enjoying my tea and my cat, questions started running through my mind:

- Do you have any idea how God feels when He looks upon you each morning?
- Do you realise that just as Zoë chose to be with you, so God delights to be with you?
- When you get up in the morning and look in the mirror, what do you see?
- When you go to bed at night are you lifted up by peace and thanksgiving or weighed down by regrets?
- As you go through your day do you sense God drawing alongside you or does He seem far off, somewhere out there in the distance?
- If you do become aware of Him is it usually with a sense of joy, or do you feel guilty that somehow you have let Him down?

I was astonished. I'd never woken up with such clear-cut and searching questions in my mind before! I realised this was God, wanting to be with me at the dawn of each new day and open me up to His love. But I knew I couldn't go through many of those questions before I'd have to answer in the negative. Deep down I did not really believe that God would actually *want* to be with me. I knew He loved me, but that often felt a distant thing, as if He was way "out there" somewhere, loving me from afar.

The concept of Him wanting to be with me seemed to speak of liking as much as loving. Could I really assert that the Creator of this Universe *liked* me? But even as I ran away from that idea, my thoughts turned towards the Song of Solomon:

> *"My dove in the clefts of the rock,*
> *   in the hiding-places on the mountainside,*
> *show me your face,*
> *   let me hear your voice;*
> *for your voice is sweet,*
> *   and your face is lovely."*
>
> (SONG OF SOLOMON 2:14)

I couldn't get these beautiful words out of my mind. God was calling me His Dove, a gentle, tender name expressing how He saw me as a person. He was open and unashamed of His desire to be with me. It wasn't enough for Him that I was just nearby, He wanted to see me and to hear what I was saying. He was calling me out of hiding into the open place of friendship. He was affirming that I was beautiful to His eye and that what I chose to share with Him really mattered.

YOU ARE BELOVED

What God said to me that morning is true for you too. God has no favourites. He watches over you and longs to bring you out of the hiding places in your life. He enjoys being with you, just as a friend enjoys the company of his/her best mate. He loves to listen and to respond to you. Listen to these amazing words from John 15:

"I've loved you the way my Father has loved me. Make yourselves at home in my love … I'm no longer calling you servants because servants don't understand what their master is thinking and planning. No, I've named you friends because I've let you in on everything I've heard from the Father."[2]

Jesus is indicating that the heart of friendship is communicating and sharing. If it is duty that motivates the friendship, it isn't a true friendship, it is servanthood. Jesus enjoyed a rich, communicative relationship with His Father in which He knew He was loved and delighted in. He says He gives you that same relationship! He loves you with the same level of love His Father loved Him. He trusts you and chooses to share with you all His Father shares with Him. This is mind boggling!

REFLECTION

Turn back to those questions that kept running through my mind. Spend a few moments thinking your own responses to them. You may like to use your journal to jot down your thoughts. Don't just put what you think should be right, put what you truly feel in your own heart. It is important that we are honest with ourselves and take our time because our answers might reveal the foundation stones of our lives and faith and our real level of relationship with God.

If you prefer it the questions could be summarised like this:

- What is my typical mindset on waking and sleeping?
- How do I see myself?
- How do I see God?
- How do I believe God sees me?
- How do I practise being with Him?

Spend some time reflecting on your responses. Are they what you expected? Do you feel you are already enjoying a daily awareness of yourself as being loved and sought after by God? Look again at the passage from the Song of Solomon and read it slowly. What does the whole passage show you about God's character? Do you think your heart picture of Him is true to this picture? Ask God to illuminate it to you by the Holy Spirit. Is there any word or phrase that particularly holds your attention? If so, jot it down and then talk to Him about it. Ask Him if there is anything He wants to tell you through that phrase. Write down any further ideas that come and then spend some time thanking Him that He has drawn close and has been speaking to you.

GOD'S PRESENCE MAKES US RADIANT

I often have the privilege of praying with someone who is in pain or struggling in some way. One of the most moving things is the transformation that comes in a person's face or posture as they are touched by the healing presence of the Lord. Just the other day there was such a lady. Her expression was dark and closed after sharing her story of rejection, her hands clenched into fists on her lap. Marilyn and I prayed for God's Spirit to reach into the wounds, to release her from bitterness and to fill her with new hope, that she would be able to see herself truly as His beloved daughter. As she sat locked and frozen, we quietly prayed in tongues welcoming and blessing the healing work of the Holy Spirit. Gradually her whole demeanour changed. Her hands unlocked and relaxed in her lap. She rested her head back against the chair, her mouth curved upwards in a gentle smile. When she eventually opened her eyes I was moved to tears by the glow of peace emanating from her.

Pause for thought

- Do you know that God's presence radiates though you?
- Ponder these verses:

> *"When Moses came down from Mount Sinai with the two tablets of the Testimony in his hands, he was not aware that his face was radiant because he had spoken with the LORD."*
>
> (EXODUS 34:29)

> *"Those who look to him are radiant;*
> *their faces are never covered with shame."*
>
> (PSALM 34:5)

ILLUMINED FROM WITHIN

Last Christmas I was given a mandle candle. I had never had one before and did not know what to expect. It just looked like an ordinary candle, a round pillar striped red and white. I lit the match and the wick flared and caught. A moment of stillness, hesitation, a wafting flame. Then joy and amazement as the candle's secret beauty burst into life – a pillar of vibrant colours melting one into the other; a rainbow glowing with life.

Yet all that beautiful light and colour was latent and hidden until a flame was touched to the wick and kindled it into life. On its own the candle was pretty enough, but ordinary. No one would guess that when lit it would glow in such an incredible way. The candle might be aware, if it had feelings, that it had a treasure inside it, that it was different and special; yet it would not be able to unearth that treasure on its own. It needed the flame from the outside, reaching into the secret place, the core of its being from where its soul stretched upwards in vulnerable longing. Once that flame

came, then life came. The candle burning, a candle transformed; the candle receiving fire, the candle giving fire; a
willing, inward melting, allowing itself to be changed from
the inside out, to become a molten pool instead of a rock;
for its strong exterior to melt in its own turn, even to
disappear, yet all the while glowing with that beautiful light.

Once I discovered the beauty of this candle it awoke a
desire in me to see it again and again. I knew that treasure
was there and it became my delight to bring that treasure
into life, to give it the gift of a flame and see the joy of the
candle receiving it and burning with it in its own right. To
see the glow of colour and light spreading around it, a star in
its orbit. And I realised that this is the love of God for us. He
sees us and recognises that there is a treasure within us. In
fact, He is the one who put it there, for did He not create us?
He sees the longing within us, the stretching up of something naked and vulnerable and yet our inability to light our
own fire, however hard we try. So He comes to us and as we
tentatively open the door of our trust and hope He reaches
in with the fire of His Spirit and sets our hearts alight.

REFLECTION

A prophetic picture – God's word of love through a candle.

The following prophecy came to me when I was prayerfully
watching the candle, together with the verse from Zephaniah
3 quoted at the end. This is God's heart for you. Read it
slowly and receptively. Allow Him to touch and bathe you
with His love. Write your responses down in your journal.

*"My dear child, when you think of My love for you, I know that
deep down in your spirit you are afraid that there will come a time
when My love for you will run out. You fear that you will only be*

able to go so far and that will be the end of it. You fear that if you let Me down too much or do or say the wrong thing too often that My love will become a thing of the past to you. But My dear child, I love you with a love that can never run out or be exhausted. My love is like a candle that will never burn out. Even the tallest and thickest of candles will burn out in the end; the wax will melt as the candle burns and the wick will be destroyed until the whole candle has been consumed. But the candle of My love is not like that. Instead the candle of My love grows bigger as it burns. The wax grows thicker and the wick grows longer. This is because the candle is burning with My love for you which I am actively feeding every day. I feed it with My delight in you and the joy I take in you. Yes, My dear child, I delight in you. I love your thoughts and your feelings. I love to know you and to cherish you. I love to take you in My arms and soothe and calm you and to just rejoice in you because you are My child. I want you to lay your head on My breast and know you are safe in a love that will never let you go. I love what you do, but most of all I love you just because you are My beloved child. As I delight in you in this way, the candle of My love for you is constantly fed and grows bigger. Whatever happens, its light will never go out. It will always burn with My love for you."

A verse to meditate upon:

"The LORD your God is with you,
  he is mighty to save.
He will take great delight in you,
  he will quiet you with his love,
  he will rejoice over you with singing."

(ZEPHANIAH 3:17)

Notes

1. Henri J.M. Nouwen, *Life of the Beloved* (Hodder & Stoughton, © 1992).
2. John 15:9, 15, MSG.

flying free
with God

living in the truth of God's healing love

CHAPTER 6

ROYAL SONS AND DAUGHTERS

Intimacy, Healing and Anointing

"Those who are led by the Spirit of God are sons of God."
(ROMANS 8:14)

A TRANSFORMING WORD OF KNOWLEDGE

Recently a lady, Jayne, shared her first experience of hearing
God's voice prophetically. She was part of the ministry team
at a big event. Before the meeting began everyone on the
team prayed together and the leader encouraged them to
listen to the Lord. Several people then shared lovely words
and insights from God, some for physical problems, others
for areas of struggle in people's lives. Jayne said how
confused she felt as she listened. She'd also had an insight,

but it didn't make any sense. She tried to dismiss it, thinking she was imagining things, but couldn't push it out of her mind. Eventually she shared it with the group: "A lady here will be wearing a fuchsia blouse." People waited for her to continue, but she had nothing more to say and felt very silly. The leader then encouraged everyone to share their words in the meeting, so again, feeling foolish, she did.

At the end Jayne was praying for those who came forward. A lady approached her, firstly slipping off her coat. She was wearing a bright pink blouse. She looked at Jayne and asked,

"Why did you mention a fuchsia blouse in the meeting?"

"I don't know!" Jayne replied. "I believe God asked me to say it, but I don't know why."

The lady glanced down at her blouse and when she looked up again she had tears in her eyes. "Tonight I put on a green blouse," she said. "I was about to leave the house but suddenly felt I should swap it for this fuchsia one. It seemed crazy as I was perfectly happy with the green one." She paused and glanced down again before continuing. "Can you pray with me?" she asked softly. "I've drifted away from God because I felt my life didn't matter to Him. But I was obviously wrong!"

LED BY THE SPIRIT

I shared this story at the start of this chapter because of its message of joy and hope. The wonder of God meeting with us in our brokenness. The tenderness of His "mother heart" in reaching someone lost and hurting. How incredible for her to realise that not only did she matter to God, but even her clothes were important enough for Him to notice! Sometimes we just don't comprehend how big and yet how extraordinarily detailed the love of God is for us. As Psalm 139 expresses,

> *"O LORD, you have searched me*
> *and you know me.*
> *You know when I sit and when I rise;*
> *you perceive my thoughts from afar.*
> *You discern my going out and my lying down;*
> *you are familiar with all my ways.*
> *Before a word is on my tongue,*
> *you know it completely, O LORD."*

(PSALM 139:1–4)

Through this word of knowledge the lady was able to let go of the lies that had crippled her faith and live once again as a beloved daughter of God. Through this same word, Jayne knew the joy that she could hear the Lord and experience being led by the Spirit, living as both a child of God and an heir together with Christ. The word of knowledge was incomprehensible to her, but she learnt through it that she didn't need to understand everything, just to trust God and step out in faith; the results were His responsibility. This reminds me of the story of God calling Ananias in the book of Acts.

> *"The Lord called to him in a vision, 'Ananias!'*
>
> *'Yes, Lord', he answered.*
>
> *The Lord told him, 'Go to the house of Judas on Straight Street and ask for a man from Tarsus named Saul, for he is praying. In a vision he has seen a man named Ananias come and place his hands on him to restore his sight.'*
>
> *'Lord,' Ananias answered, 'I have heard many reports about this man and all the harm he has done to your saints...'*
>
> *But the Lord said to Ananias, 'Go! This man is my chosen instrument...'*
>
> *Then Ananias went..."*

(ACTS 9:10–13, 15, 17 précis)

Through this Holy Spirit inspired conversation with the Lord, Ananias took significant steps into what it meant to be a Kingdom son. Like Jayne, he had no idea why the Lord should tell him to do such a crazy thing. After all, this would not just make him look a fool, it was positively dangerous! But the essence of true Kingdom sonship is trust. God wants us to be stepping out with a deep heart trust that He knows what He is doing and incredibly has chosen us to work in partnership with Him. We are sons and heirs with all His resources at our disposal to do His works. But the most important resource is our willingness to love and trust Him. As we step out in obedient trust we will know Kingdom joy. Jesus tells us,

> *"As the Father has loved me, so have I loved you. Now remain in my love. If you obey my commands, you will remain in my love, just as I have obeyed my Father's commands and remain in his love. I have told you this so that my joy may be in you and that your joy may be complete."*
>
> (JOHN 15:9–11)

THE WONDER OF THE GIFTS OF THE SPIRIT

The power and discernment of God, made known to us through the Holy Spirit-given spiritual gifts, reaches into our lives in deeper ways than mere human words can ever do. This is why it is so key that we listen and follow His promptings, rather than just relying on our own understanding. My friend, Lilian, and I prayed with a lady, Anne, who had many deep regrets. Christians had told her that God forgave her, but she couldn't forgive herself. We prayed together and then Lilian shared a vision from God in which she saw a very large blackboard with Anne's life history written down it in a long list. Anne was standing in front of it

looking at it. Lilian then saw the Lord come with a large
board duster. He rubbed it all out and said, "Now you are
the only one that knows what was there. If you can let it go,
it's gone."

Although this tied in with what Christians had counselled
before, the vision was graphic and had an immediacy about
it that reached Anne's spirit. She wrote to us afterwards to
say that now a new flame of hope had been ignited in her
heart.

Pause to reflect

- Have you ever sensed God communicating to you about
  a person or a situation or asked Him to do so?
- How did the communication come to you? For example,
  sudden knowledge, an awareness you should do or say
  something, a vision or prophecy or Bible verse?
- Did you do anything about it? And if so, what were the
  results, if known?
- Thank Him for His wonderful works of love and that
  He equips you as son and heir to share in them.
- Spend a few moments asking Jesus to fill you afresh with
  the Holy Spirit who brings you these wonderful gifts and
  ask Him to increase your expectancy that He will speak
  to you in this way.

GROWING INTO SONSHIP

Am I blind or not?

Some years ago I flew to the USA to visit some friends. It
was my first solo flight and I was anxious about managing. I
knew that with my deafness I would not hear any announce-
ments, and with my eyesight I would not be able to read the
information screens! Would I end up in Antarctica rather
than America?

On the advice of Marilyn, who was used to the procedure, I reluctantly decided to ask for special assistance. This was a huge step for me as I'd spent much of my life denying that I had any problem at all, especially with my sight. I could walk couldn't I, albeit in a rather wobbly way! So surely I couldn't be classified as disabled like those waiting with me at the special needs desk, zimmers, crutches and wheelchairs at their sides? But to my chagrin, it didn't take many moments for the official to agree that I indeed merited special assistance and soon my "buggy" arrived to collect me.

If this term "buggy" conjures up for you the image of a pushchair for toddlers, an airport assistance buggy is like an open topped car. You either face forwards, next to the driver, or backwards, facing the crowds who've just had to dodge out of your way! A tall pole topped with a flashing light and a loud, beeping siren complete the "inconspicuous" effect.

On that first occasion I hated it and tried my best to look like I was just an airport official on business. (Nowadays I enjoy the buggy experience. The drivers seem to have such fun whirling in and out of the crowds at top speed!)

But the climax of my "assisted" flight to America came when landing at John F. Kennedy Airport. I had asked for assistance to find the correct baggage reclaim conveyor. When I reached the door of the plane an official was waiting for me and held out his arm to guide me.

"I don't need guiding," I said. "I just can't read the signs, but I can see OK to follow you."

"But we have you down as blind", he said, "so take my arm and let me guide you safely."

"I'm not blind, just partially sighted," I said rather indignantly. "I really don't need guiding. If you go ahead I will follow you."

He shrugged, turned round and walked ahead of me. I

was pleased to have "won" and quickly stepped down. Unfortunately, I didn't see the ridge at the edge of the ramp and tripped over it crashing into the official's back and propelling him forwards several feet! When he'd regained his balance (and mine) he unsmilingly offered me his arm again. I didn't say anything. I just took it. On this occasion at least, I needed guiding!

GUIDING INTO THE TRUTH OF WHO WE ARE IN CHRIST

My flying experience that day speaks to me about our relationship with the truth of who we are in Christ. I was in quite a double-minded place on that journey. I was anxious about not managing on my own – which was a true assessment, but nothing to be ashamed of and had a great solution in the form of airport help; embarrassed about looking disabled and needing help – which was a silly misconception coming out of a place of shame; and trying to appear what I *wasn't* – which was a lack of acceptance of myself as I *was*.

IS THIS A PICTURE OF WHERE WE ARE IN CHRIST?

Most of us look at who we are through very foggy glasses. We know we have weaknesses, but instead of viewing them as a means of leaning on God's incredible grace, we act ashamed and may even use them to disqualify ourselves from being true participants in God's kingdom. Moses did this when God called him to lead the Israelites into freedom. Out of his sense of inadequacy an amazing conversation ensued which reveals God's mercy in meeting us in our broken places yet, in His love, refusing to let us hide there. Exodus 3:11–4:13:

Moses	God
"Who am I to go?	I will be with you, I have sent you.
Who are You?	I AM WHO I AM.
What shall I say?	I AM has sent me to you.
They won't believe me.	What is that in your hand?
I've got a stammer.	Who gave man his mouth?
I can't do it, Lord, not me!	Your brother Aaron is already coming. I will help you both."

In his book *The Supernatural Ways of Royalty*,[1] Kris Vallotton tells how God drew his attention to Moses' life as a prince in the Egyptian royal courts and how, through those forty years of living as a prince, God had been preparing him to understand the ways of royalty, building that into his make-up in readiness for when he was to lead the new nation. Yet, in this moment of encounter with God, Moses forgets his princely foundation. All he can feel is shame and confusion. Behind all the excuses is the "fact" of his badness. He'd already tried to fulfil his sense of call to save his own people and had messed up big time in the process. Forty years on the run in the desert had kept him safe from execution, but had not dealt with his shame. God's call drove him to his knees as he was pulled on the one hand by the incredible mercy and purpose of God and on the other by his own self-despising spirit.

BE ENCOURAGED – MOSES WAS SO LIKE US!

I feel encouraged by Moses' story. Like many of us he felt so inferior and used his weaknesses as an excuse. I identify with him and then am awed as I see how God perseveres. He is grieved, even angry at Moses' lack of faith, but He won't be put off. He knows what He has destined Moses for and the princely gifts He has given Moses to fulfil that calling. In holy love He allows Moses to state His case. He listens and responds. He shows him He has already seen his need for help and is bringing Aaron. But He doesn't mollycoddle Moses or sympathetically allow him to stay cocooned in inadequacy. The lesson He teaches Moses and all of us, is to throw himself in all his weakness onto God and dare to trust Him for the results.

Out of the Bog

Feelings of shame and inadequacy are like a muddy bog pulling us into the depths and trapping us. It is the devil's lies that act as the downward suction. He grips us in our weakest areas and reminds us of negative experiences and past failures. He accuses us and constantly seeks to rob and belittle us. But the devil is defeated through Jesus' death and resurrection. He no longer has any rights over us, unless we ourselves give him those rights again by believing his lies rather than trusting in God's freeing truth. We have to make an ongoing choice to believe and live in the truth of who God is and what He says about us. Making that choice will break the power of the devil's lies. As James teaches us,

"Resist the devil, and he will flee from you."

(JAMES 4:7)

Onto the Firm Ground of God's Truth

To trust and focus on the truth of God's love and power is the choice Peter made when he took his first step out of the boat and walked on the water towards Jesus. If our inadequacies and fears stop us from doing things that are humanly possible, how much more will they stop us from attempting the humanly *impossible*? Yet, it is to the realm of the humanly impossible that God calls and equips us as His sons and heirs. Peter, like Moses, was empowered to do the impossible as he looked to Jesus alone. We too can hear Jesus calling us to come to Him. As we respond to Him in faith we will experience Him empowering us to leave that boat and all it represents of false safety and imprisoning lies and live in the kingdom dimension of radical love and possibility.

JOY IN STEPPING OUT OF SHAME

In the early years of my Christian life I always felt awkward and physically rigid because of my coordination difficulties and the abuse I'd experienced with its effects of fear and shame. I longed to raise my hands in worship, but there was such a paralysing sense of exposure in lifting my arms away from my body. I loved the beauty and power of dance but it was an "impossibility" to even imagine trying it myself. I remember when my church had an evening of worship and we were encouraged to try putting simple interpretative movements to the words. Everyone seemed so caught up in the joy of this, but I felt overwhelmed by panic. I ran out of church back to my home and hid in the bathroom crying. My friend Siân found me and prayed that the Lord Jesus would heal the past traumas and set me free to worship in the way I longed. God gave her a picture of me in a beautiful ballerina's dress twirling with arms outstretched and she felt He was saying that I was going to dance, but I couldn't believe this. It seemed so impossible and I decided she was just trying to comfort me.

But years later while with Marilyn at a conference led by Jennifer Rees Larcombe, a professional dancer had planned to lead a dance workshop. But one morning she announced she could no longer do it. Later I said to Marilyn, "It's such a shame about the dance workshop, so many were looking forward to it!"

Marilyn said something ridiculous: "Why don't you do it?"

I burst out laughing. How could I possibly lead a dance workshop? I had never danced in my life. I couldn't hear, was wobbly as a jelly and although much more healed, I was still very nervous of being physically expressive.

But I could not forget Marilyn's suggestion. When I went to bed her words went round and round in my mind. It was crazy! How could someone like me who had never even danced, *lead* a group? What would be the point of it? Everyone would think it as daft as I did myself. No, we would just have to abandon the idea of having a dance workshop.

But as much as I tried to rationalise how silly an idea it was, I could not get away from it. Deep down I knew it was God. I told Him every reason against it I could think of. But suddenly the thought came that maybe others were as fearful as me of being physically expressive? Would it therefore help them if they had a leader who felt the same? With that I fell asleep and when I woke the next morning I knew I was going to do it.

That first dance workshop was an amazing experience. We were such a motley group. There was a blind lady and another who walked with a stick, a very old lady and one suffering acute depression. Hardly any had danced before so we were all fearful and very stiff. We decided to use one of Marilyn's songs, *Overflow of Worship*, as I knew the words and had a sense of the tune. We thought of simple movements to express the meanings of the words and then put them together as a whole group. We performed it in the fun night and were so scared and self-conscious. It could not have been called a polished dance by any stretch of the imagination and yet ... it was beautiful. Afterwards many watching said how deeply moved and inspired they had been.

For me, and I believe for several in that group, it was a pivotal moment. To use my body to express beauty, love, worship and emotion was an incredible release. And as we danced, I realised something wonderful, that God Himself was blessed by the love we were offering Him in our weakness. He alone knew how hard it was, yet the fact that we had sacrificially stepped out gave Him deep joy and opened the door to the Kingdom of Heaven.

Since then I have led dance workshops in most of our conferences and also perform solo in Marilyn's concerts. Many have taken part in the workshops. It is deeply humbling when people who are ill or disabled or who struggle with loss or emotional pain still do their utmost to physically express God's love and beauty. Again and again audiences have commented how moved they are and challenged to step out of their own comfort zones. Here is a comment from a friend, Debbie:

> "When I watch the dances I feel very humbled because it is normally people who aren't especially gifted in dancing that take part and that takes courage. I find it really moving. It is also good for those taking part (me included) to realise that you can do these things and don't have to be an expert dancer."

Nessa, a blind friend, said:

> "It was great. It lifted me up to God. I found great release in my spirit being able to express myself in that way to God. I feel these things cause me to be with the Lord. I certainly never thought I'd be worshipping like that! It showed me what God has done in giving me freedom from being an introvert and it made me feel equal with sighted people too!"

Emotionally, I still find it hard, especially when performing on stage. I am very aware, with Marilyn being a professional musician, that humanly it is a bizarre thing to have a wobbly, out-of-time dancer alongside her. Yet I know that God wants me to do it and each time I feel such a joy in loving Him and testifying through my movements to His incredible love and healing.

Pause to ponder...

- Our own human words of sympathy often just confirm how bad a problem is and draw us into a cosy place of hopelessness! God's responses however, such as to Moses, make us look upwards and outwards instead of downwards and inwards.
- Are there times when your own sense of weakness has become a big mountain that you've hidden behind?
- Have you sensed God calling you to see yourself differently or to do something for Him?
- How have you responded?
- What has it made you feel?

CREATED IN LOVE TO BE A REFLECTION OF GOD'S LOVE

I wrote the following prayer poem, *Creator without Apology*, when I was staying at a retreat centre at the end of what had been a very difficult year. Repeatedly, I'd come face to face with issues that did their utmost to convince me that I was a complete failure. I was even doubting my Christian experience and call to ministry because of listening to all these negative lies. The enemy is very subtle and knows how to make lies masquerade as truths and then he sneaks in and robs us.

On the first day of the retreat I went into a room called "Creation", full of beautiful plants and a huge banner of a waterfall. As I gazed into the riot of leaves and flowers I became aware of God as Creator. He was overflowing with pleasure at all He had made. I sensed Him whispering into my heart,

"Look closely at the incredible beauty and care that I have lavished on each tiny part of these plants. Some parts are not even seen but are still vital. Everything is significant and matters beyond measure to Me because I created them to fulfil My purposes. How much more joyfully and beautifully did I create you?"

I was amazed. It was as if it was the first time I had ever truly heard that God had created me in love. I gazed at the beauty before me. It seemed impossible to think that I could be more beautiful to God than these. The pain of feeling a nobody was so strong in my heart, yet I knew God had drawn very close and wanted not just to comfort me but to lift me out of that past place of woundedness and slavery into the eternally true place of beloved daughter and heir. I cried as I said to Him, "Lord, I want so much to live in the truth of who I am in You." As I prayed I wrote it down and it became a conversation with Him as I sensed His answers. I was not thinking about my writing – it was a personal and powerful encounter with Creator God. It was only afterwards as I read it that I realised it was beautiful and quite poetic.

I have since read it aloud several times and seen God free those caught in the web of self-despising and draw them out into the freedom of His truth.

Creator without Apology
Lord, I feel such a sense of apology.
I have seen Your creation today
The glory of the autumn leaves
Revealing the gold of Your glory.
I have seen the beauty of the plants
And felt the joy of Your creation,
That You put the stamp of who You are on each and
    every living thing
Without apology.

An extravagance of colour, shape, texture and smell
Each tiny leaf or bud, twig or root,
Itself, gladly,
Without apology.
But then I sensed You say to me:
"In as far as these things reflect My beauty,
They are nothing compared to you."
And I recoiled, for how could that possibly be?
It is my greatest longing to be someone who reflects
    Your glory
Yet I cannot seem to think of me
Without apology.
Deep down I feel like a jumble of things thrown
    together
Rather haphazardly
A kind of mistake, neither this nor that.
An embarrassment has become my identity
You say, "Could I have created My child with less
    passion and joy
To be less beautiful than a flower, a bird or a tree?
As beautiful as they are and revealing of My splendour
They cannot talk with Me.
I have made you to be joined in love
To know and be part of Me
Through all that you are and do
To thus reveal My beauty."
But the shame that runs through me like thread through
    a cloth
Draws me down and away.
If I were anyone else I would accept that as true
But not as me.
But deep in my heart I hear Him still,
"Tracy, Tracy,"
And His voice is warm and full of love,
Reaching in to me.

I long to uncurl from my foetal ball
And let Him draw the shame thread from me
And He hears my longing and speaks again,
"Child, accept the gift I have made you to be."
And this is the door that I need to go through
Into all that God has for me.
It seems heavy, dark, impenetrable
But He has offered me the key.
I do not know how to use it
For the shame thread blinds and binds me,
Draws me inward and grips my heart.
So accepting myself as a gift
Seems an impossibility.
What about my deafness, slowness, lack of ability?
Surely they are not gifts, they constantly rob me!
And in my anger I echo the words I've heard,
You're just pathetic, a useless liability,
But His voice comes again, warm and even laughing,
"Child, don't let your wounds blind you to the artist
And limit the richness of My creativity."
And I hear and am stilled and stand at that door.
And realise He is standing there with me.
And I turn to Him and ask, as no plant can do,
"Please forgive me my blindness and for mocking
    Your art.
Please help me take and use that key.
Because I really do want to be free."[2]

CHILD, ACCEPT THE GIFT I'VE MADE YOU TO BE

When we deny ourselves, we are ultimately denying Jesus who has chosen to live within us and to make our lives His home. We are actually temples of the Holy Spirit. What Jesus was asking that day was for me to live my life in the confident trust that He was living within me with His light shining through me. This is true and vital for all of us to take into our hearts. It is the essence of our son/daughtership. We may feel weak in ourselves, but that very weakness can become a treasure in His hands. As Paul teaches us,

"But we have this treasure in jars of clay to show that this all-surpassing power is from God and not from us."
(2 CORINTHIANS 4:7)

He wants to touch the people around us with His love and draw them to Him. He seeks to do that through you and me, even in our very weaknesses. He brought this home to me in an amazing way through the words of two people on the very same day I wrote the above poem. First, Mags, my retreat leader, said, "Trace, it's important you know that when you get to Heaven you are going to be welcomed by Jesus and a huge crowd of people whose lives you have touched in an amazing way even when not knowing them."

Later in the day, Chris, a fellow retreatant, said to me, "Your disabilities are a great gift, you reflect the beauty of God. You somehow help me to see God just by being the person you are. In my journal I have written how you radiate God ... believe in yourself. You are very special."

I don't think either Mags or Chris will ever know how significant their words were. It had been a subconscious fear for so long that when I reach Heaven I will find I have disappointed God. Yet now I was hearing that Jesus would be there to welcome me plus many people whose lives I'd touched with God's love. Hearing this was as if Mags and Chris had been privy to my earlier experience in the Creation room and were confirming all that God had been saying to me. Neither of them realised they were speaking prophetic-ally, with divine accuracy, into that immediate area of God's work in my life. Yet that was the case and I was filled with wonder. They were speaking out of true sonship, hearing the heart of the Father for me and bringing deep encouragement. Thus Paul teaches us that the gifts of the Holy Spirit are for encouragement of the body of Christ:

> *"Everyone who prophesies speaks to men for their strengthening, encouragement and comfort."*
>
> (1 CORINTHIANS 14:3)

This was what had happened as they unknowingly prophesied over me. I was encouraged and awed. Their words enabled me to step more fully into accepting myself as beloved daughter of God. But in sharing those words they had themselves stepped forward in their own holy anointing as royal daughters. This is the glorious fruit of allowing God to heal and release us into who we are in Him. We become a united Body, radiating His love and powerfully giving away His life-changing encouragement.

REFLECT

- Make some time to be quiet with God and prayerfully read through the *Creator without Apology* poem again.
- Do any parts of it speak to you personally?
- Is any "shame thread" running through your life, holding you back from knowing the truth about yourself? Can you tell Jesus about it and give Him permission to draw it out of you?
- Can you recognise and accept that you too have the treasure of God's life within you, that your very weaknesses are gifts in His hands?
- He showed me that was a key which I ultimately prayed would be turned in my life. Can you pray that same prayer?

- Note down your responses and take time to talk to God about them? Maybe, like Mags and Chris' words to me, someone has spoken encouragement to you. Thank God for that and receive it afresh.

Follow Me
and I Will Make You . . .

"As Jesus was walking beside the sea of Galilee, he saw two brothers, Simon called Peter and his brother Andrew. They were casting a net into the lake, for they were fishermen. 'Come, follow me,' Jesus said, 'and I will make you fishers of men.' At once they left their nets and followed Him."

(MATTHEW 4:18–20)

Whenever I read this passage it always stops me in my tracks. It fills me with a sense of excitement and adventure. Yet it is incredibly brief in its description and arouses many questions. Why did Jesus stop by and choose these two particular men? What did they see in Him that made them step away from what they had always known and the people they had always been with, to follow this man who was already stirring controversy? What enabled them to make that choice?

The key is Jesus' invitation for them to discover the potential of what they could truly become. They were used to a particular level of being and attaining. They knew their skills, their strengths and weaknesses, but their horizons had narrowed to the level of their experience. Now Jesus with His few pithy words was opening those horizons and awakening the whisper in their hearts that there was more to live for and attain, more to experience. Such a realisation can be exhilarating! Yet sometimes we allow ourselves to be exhilarated, but then go no further.

The Call to Follow

Jesus said to them, *"Come, follow me and I will make you..."* Jesus was asking them to take their eyes off what they already knew and dare to go along a new path. For them the path involved leaving their present lifestyles and literally following Him. Sometimes we can feel it must have been much easier when Jesus was physically there. But Jesus was not talking about walking along the road with Him! Thousands of people did that every day, but only a few became His disciples. Jesus was talking about intimacy. He was calling them to live in a different dimension – the dimension of love fuelling the desire to listen and act on what is heard; to see and to be changed. And as they hear God's words of truth, faith is born and grows and they are empowered to live in Kingdom Sonship.

As Paul teaches the Romans:

"Those who are led by the Spirit of God are sons of God."
(ROMANS 8:14)

Remember what God spoke into my heart that frosty morning in the field? *"The creation waits in eager expectation for the sons of God to be revealed"* (Romans 8:19). God gave man authority to work in partnership with Him in governing the created world. But man forfeited that by listening to and believing the lies of the devil instead of the glorious truths of God. Now, through Jesus, we are restored and have the opportunity once again to listen to the true voice, to follow the Holy Spirit and thus impact the very fabric of this world with the Kingdom of Heaven. Not following the Holy Spirit in a robotic way like machines, but as sons, daughters and joint heirs with Christ. The following story illustrates this.

HEALING AND RESTORATION

Chrissie was a young woman who came to one of our conferences and had prayer with team members Ron and Val. Chrissie told them how she had been happily married for a few years to a loving Christian husband. They had tried for some time to start a family but to no avail. Failed IVF treatment was followed by a miscarriage. Finally, they were told that it wouldn't be possible for them to have children.

Shortly after, the husband announced that he was leaving her as he had found another partner who was already pregnant with his child.

This was a total bombshell to Chrissie. It destroyed her self-esteem, her confidence, and almost her faith. When she came for prayer she had little hope left and was a fragile and much damaged young lady.

Ron and Val sat holding her hands not knowing quite what to pray for. As they began to seek God's face, Val felt God saying, "Tell Chrissie that she will have many children in time to come." At the same time Ron received a picture of Jesus sitting in a garden with children crawling all over Him. It had the text underneath, "Suffer little children to come to Me for of such is the Kingdom of Heaven." As Ron watched, the picture changed from Jesus to Chrissie. This seemed to confirm Val's message.

Ron and Val rather fearfully told Chrissie these words from God and prayed to bless her and release her into all God had for her. Before leaving they gave Chrissie their address just in case she wanted to get in touch in the future.

Many months later a letter arrived from Chrissie. It said:

"Hi, remember me, Chrissie? You prayed for me and told me wonderful, unbelievable things that God had in store for me. Well, I picked myself up and began to believe again, and after being asked to relieve some folk who were travelling to Romania several times a year to help support a children's work, I went. I fell in love with the leader of the work and we are soon to be married. When I move to Romania I will have more children to look after than I can think of. Thank you, dear God!"

If that wasn't amazing enough, Ron and Val had a further letter from Chrissie telling them she was now married and incredibly had just given birth to her own lovely little boy!

"THOSE WHO ARE LED BY THE SPIRIT OF GOD ARE SONS OF GOD"

The foundation of this lovely story of restoration is that both Ron and Val and Chrissie herself were all led by the Holy Spirit. Ron and Val had no idea how to pray for Chrissie. In their weakness they could only listen to God in the hope they would be given wisdom. Wisdom came in the form of the spiritual insights each received and shared. It is not always right to immediately speak out what God gives. Sometimes He just wants us to pray – for example, Jesus heard of his friend's Lazarus terminal illness, but in prayer sensed the Holy Spirit telling Him to wait until Lazarus had actually died rather than go immediately and heal him. As He listened He knew by revelation that God would raise Lazarus from the dead. He also knew He must not speak out this knowledge. It would be made known by the witnessing of the miracle itself. So instead of sharing it, He treasured God's secret plan in His heart. The resulting miracle was awesome in displaying God's supreme glory and power. It brought many to faith and acted as a prophetic statement of Jesus' own approaching death and resurrection (John 11:1–45).

God will always give wisdom to know how to act on His insights. Ron and Val knew it was right for them to share with Chrissie the divine insight they had been given. Chrissie then followed the Spirit by actively believing what she had heard, as she described in her letter:

> "You prayed for me and told me wonderful, unbeliev-able things that God had in store for me. *Well, I picked myself up and began to believe again . . .*"

Chrissie had every reason to doubt their words and be cynical. Instead she chose to believe that God loved her despite all the brokenness she was experiencing. She chose to believe He had promised to do something wonderful. Her belief and active trust empowered her to move on in the hope of those words being fulfilled. That hope and faith opened the door to the Kingdom of Heaven and the miracle of dreams fulfilled.

THINK ABOUT THESE THINGS

In Philippians 4:8 Paul encourages the new Christians to consciously fix their minds on the positive things, to think about them and ponder them.

> *"Finally, brothers, whatever is true, whatever is noble, whatever is right, whatever is pure, whatever is lovely, whatever is admirable — if anything is excellent or praiseworthy — think about such things."*

The natural bent of our minds is to focus on the negative. Marilyn once did a concert where the organiser had put comment forms out on the chairs. At the end of the concert her assistant took them back to their hosts in order to go through them with Marilyn. 99% of the forms were very complimentary saying what a blessing and joy the concert had been. One, however, said something like: "A wasted opportunity. Marilyn sings about the change Jesus brings, but she needs to ask Him to change her first!"

Marilyn was totally shocked. Although her assistant carried on reading the rest of the forms, all of which were full of praise, Marilyn kept harking back to that one negative one. She went over and over why this person may have made such a comment. What she had done to upset him so much? Maybe he was a very gloomy, bitter kind of person. Should she stop doing concerts if they were having such a bad effect...? She became more and more upset. Eventually she asked who had written it so she could pray for them! When her friend read her the person's name there was a stunned silence, then Marilyn burst out laughing. It was the name of a comic character that she had made up for fun events. Her assistant had filled out the form in this character's name and slipped it into the pile as a joke!

Although that story had a humorous outcome it illustrates an important point. We focus so readily on the negatives. It's as if they carry the weight of fact and truth to us, whereas the positives we often dismiss with a, "Yes, but..."

A Pollyanna Attitude?

In his letter to the Philippians, Paul gives us an important key to enable us to break free from this negative pattern. He tells us to make a deliberate choice to think about the good things, the things that are noble or excellent and which lift our hearts to praise. Where it is often automatic in us to dwell on hurts and negatives, Paul tells us to deliberately turn our thoughts onto the positives. But that raises the question, does that just mean positive thinking? A Pollyanna attitude? If that is the case our response might easily be, "Get real!" For while there is some merit in being optimistic and always looking on the bright side, it can often be just a vague hope rooted in our denial of what is really happening and as such can be very irritating and even destructive!

Paul's counsel goes much further than just practising positive thinking. The reason we can think about the noble, good and lovely things is that they are descriptions of who God is, how He can be seen and known, and the truth and life-changing power of His promises and words. This means that as we choose to think of Him in this way, noticing all the lovely things around us and recognising they are of Him, our spirits are opened up like flowers opening to the warmth of the sun. We then enter a place where we can be healed and released from the power of the negatives. It does not mean denying our pain, but from that broken place we can see that God is there and that He *is* good and has good plans for us.

This life-giving truth is made alive to us in the story of Abraham and the promise he received from God that he would have his own son. Impossible dreams becoming possible because of our incredible God who draws us into unimagined dimensions of faith and transformation.

FACING THE FACTS IN HOPE

"Against all hope, Abraham in hope believed and so became the father of many nations, just as it had been said to him, 'So shall your offspring be.' Without weakening in his faith, he faced the fact that his body was as good as dead – since he was about a hundred years old – and that Sarah's womb was also dead. Yet he did not waver through unbelief regarding the promise of God, but was strengthened in his faith and gave thanks to God, being fully persuaded that God had power to do what he had promised."

(ROMANS 4:18–21)

This is no Pollyanna attitude, but a true working out of what it means in everyday life to choose to believe and trust in the promises of God rather than in the negatives. Our negatives often seem to have an aura of "truth" and "fact" about them and for Abraham that was certainly the case. What could be more hopeless than the fact that (a) Sarah had been infertile all her life, and (b) they were both far too old for it to be physically possible for a child to be conceived. As Paul puts it succinctly in Romans, their bodies were "as good as dead"!

So what did Abraham do? How did he make that journey from despair to conviction?

It seems that as Paul sought God for understanding about the familiar story of Abraham, he received divine insight. He saw that, *"without weakening in his faith, Abraham faced the fact that his body was as good as dead . . . "* I love the way Paul writes this, "Abraham faced the fact . . . "

The Pollyanna mentality often means denial of our true pain with an attitude of, "Don't worry, everything is OK." Abraham accepted that things were not OK. He looked at the facts and assessed the situation. Humanly there really was no way they could have a child, it was impossible. There was no bright side they could look on, just a blank wall.

But then from that position Abraham made a choice and the choice was to turn round and put his back to that wall and look in a different direction. Not in the sense of just pretending everything was OK, but with a mind, spirit, soul and body choice to look at God rather than at the human impossibility. The result: the miracle of his son Isaac and the birthing of the new nation that you and I are citizens of, and as citizens are royal sons and daughters of the Most High King. It is an eternal, global nation without boundaries or dynasties, whose culture and language is life-changing intimate love, hope and faith in God the Father, Son and Holy Spirit.

STEPPING OUT OF THE CHRYSALIS
AND BECOMING TRUE CHILDREN OF GOD

Mark tells the story of the woman who touched the edge of Jesus' robe in her longing to be healed. Her haemorrhaging disease was a condition that made her a social outcast as well as chronically weak and ill (Mark 5:24–34).

She struggled constantly with despair, hopelessness and the effects of extreme rejection. She was destitute as her search for healing had stripped her of every resource. She felt less than a person yet within her there was a hope that refused to die. Deep down she knew she was not meant to live this way; there must be an answer. One day the rumour came to her of Jesus and the healings that were changing the lives of so many. Her all but buried hope flickered into life and out of her anguished heart cry she fought her way through the recoiling crowds to touch His robe. It was all she could do, but it was her first step out of hiddenness and shame into the healing she longed for – not just physical restoration, but a heart set free to know the joy of belonging and being loved. And Jesus gave that to her. He called her out from her hiding place in the crowd. He brought her shame into the light and gently lifted it from her. He affirmed her and gave her a new name: Daughter.

> "[Jesus] *said to her, 'Daughter, your faith has healed you. Go in peace.'* "
>
> (MARK 5:34)

From that moment she started to live as a different woman, the true woman and daughter she was created to be by her loving Heavenly Father.

A few years ago I was running a fun, "colour me beautiful" colours and make-up workshop at a conference.

I needed to demonstrate autumn colours and prayed God would lead me to choose someone who would be blessed in being picked out.

My eye was drawn to a lady at the back called Jean. She seemed an extremely unlikely choice as her body language was very fearful. But I couldn't get her out of my mind. I asked her if she would like the experience. She hesitated for a long moment and then nodded and came up.

I replaced her dull blacks and greys with rich gold and amber scarves then applied make-up. The effect was astonishing. I had never seen her smile before, but when everyone told her how fantastic she looked, a most beautiful smile lit up her face.

Later in the sharing time Jean stood up in front of us all and shared how for many years she had felt so badly about herself, because of childhood abuse, that she covered herself regularly with rubbish and human excrement. When she came to the conference she was desperate. She longed to know herself truly as the daughter of God and be healed of these terrible wounds and their effects. I wept as she shared how she had come to the beauty time intending to just sit invisibly at the back. She was stunned when I picked her, out of all the people, to demonstrate on. She wanted to run out the room, but something inside told her this was God's answer to her prayer and against all natural impulses she said yes.

We were all crying now, as with that same beautiful smile we'd seen earlier, she looked slowly round at us and said,

"Being chosen, broke something in me that told me I was just rubbish and gave me the strength to come out and be touched by love. As I was made up and adorned in those beautiful colours I heard God whispering to me, *This is the real you, Jean, you are My princess.'* "

REFLECTION

- Spend some moments reflecting on these stories of Abraham and the two women. Are there areas in your life where you have almost given up because they seem like a blank wall, impossible to change?
- Allow God to breathe new hope into your spirit. When you can, tell Him you choose to turn your back on that blank wall and look instead to Him and hear, instead of the old negatives, His dynamic healing words of power and life.

PRAYER OF THANKFULNESS

"Thank You, dear Father, that You make the impossible possible. Lord, You are faithful and good and make all things new. Thank You for the truth of Your words and for the power of what Jesus has done for me on the cross. Thank You that You heal, restore and free me to truly be Your royal child and heir. Amen."

Notes
1. *The Supernatural Ways of Royalty* by Kris Vallotton with Bill Johnson, © Destiny Image Inc., 2006.
2. *Creator without Apology* by Tracy Williamson, 2006.

CONCLUSION

I have written this book out of my growing wonder that I was created to be the beloved daughter of God, living in intimate relationship with Him; not trapped like a caterpillar in a chrysalis, but flying free and alive.

You too are on that journey of discovering you are a beautiful butterfly flying free with God. Whatever life has made you feel about yourself, you are His beloved child and His love draws you into wholeness and freedom.

There was a time in my Christian life when I believed I would never experience what it meant to feel loved by God. I knew so much in my head but my heart felt hard and locked up. How could I change? What new steps did I need to take or ministry did I need to receive?

What I have discovered, more wonderful than any methods or forms of ministry, is the God who constantly loves us as Saviour, Father and Friend. He comes to us in our brokenness; He walks alongside us, sharing in our pain. He cares, He feels, and He willingly carries every part of it, even to His own death, such is the height and depth of His incredible love.

Yet, in that same love He knows what He has created us to be. He sees inside us the beauty of His own image, however obscured by pain or sin it has become. In gentle power He calls us by name and speaks His words of life and freedom, joy and wholeness, peace and forgiveness. In loving perseverance He draws us out of dark captivity into the light and sets us free to fly with Him.

All of this involves us taking steps. I have described some of them throughout this book: maybe steps of renouncing the devil's lies and choosing to believe the true words of God; steps of facing our buried pain and giving it to Jesus; steps of forgiveness and of self-acceptance; steps of refusing to hide any longer behind the mountain of our fears, but to dare to live in the power of God's love and resources.

We will all have unique steps to take on our journey to flying free with God. The key is that He knows what those steps are and will lead you, as He is leading me, into that place where you truly know you are loved and were created by Him to live as His beloved son and daughter. I am not at the end of my journey yet and won't be until I meet Him face to face. But I am sharing that journey with Him in my everyday experience of life.

Through His work in my life, I know the joy of being loved and giving that love away again. I know the peace of receiving His cleansing and comfort and the exhilaration of hearing Him whisper to show me someone else who also needs that priceless gift of peace. I am secure in my heart that whenever I fall into the trap of pain or sin, He will come and in His mercy show me the way to freedom again. He sets me free to fly with Him, not just in one, easily forgotten flash of experience, but in a daily reality of learning to live in the growing love and anointing of intimacy with Him. It is out of that intimacy that healing comes.

I pray this book has helped you to experience His incredible love and to live in the truth of it. May you know the joy of flying free with God, becoming the royal sons and daughters that you truly are.

ABOUT THE AUTHOR

Tracy Williamson was born in 1964 in North East London. At the age of two she became ill with encephalitis, which left her deaf and partially sighted with coordination difficulties. The hearing loss was not fully discovered until Tracy was twelve, which meant that she was often thought to be a slow learner. When Tracy was seven, her father died of cancer. Soon a new father came into the family. He turned out to be a violent tempered man who had a damaging effect throughout Tracy's teen years.

These childhood traumas had a huge negative impact on Tracy's life and she became very introverted and depressed. Despite that and her deafness, she pushed forward in her academic achievements, becoming a wide reader and gaining GCSE and A-Levels, excelling in English. When she was eighteen she was offered a place at what is now Hertfordshire University to take a teaching degree in the hope of becoming a teacher of the deaf. Tracy's first year at college was fraught as she came to realise that she couldn't leave her past behind. She also learned that teaching of small children was not right for her.

After a long period of anguished soul-searching Tracy made the decision to give up her dream of teaching the deaf and transferred to a BA Degree in English Literature and Education. This whole process made her desperate for real answers and help in her life and after many conversations with Christian fellow students she became a Christian in June 1983. Tracy then went on to complete her degree, gaining a 2.1 (Hons) in June 1985.

MINISTRY

In that same year, prior to forging a career with the visually impaired, Tracy met with blind singer/songwriter Marilyn Baker and a deep bond of friendship formed between them. Marilyn's assistant left in January 1986 and Marilyn asked Tracy to help her out temporarily. It soon became apparent, however, that God was calling Tracy to the ministry and she gave up her proposed course to become Marilyn's personal assistant in April 1986. She is still in this ministry today.

TRACY'S ROLE

Initially Tracy's main role was to be a practical support and administrative assistant to Marilyn. However, it soon became clear that God had anointed Tracy with gifts of communication. Beginning with sharing her testimony in concerts, Tracy then began to receive prophetic words for individuals and churches. As her prophetic gifting developed, Tracy realised how few people expected God to speak to them personally. This led to her volunteering to do a workshop on listening to God at a conference led by Jennifer Rees Larcombe in 1993. The workshop was a great success and ultimately led to the publication of her first book *The Voice of the Father* which was published by Hodder and Stoughton in 1996. Since then Tracy has written a number of articles promoting Marilyn's albums for various Christian publications. She has also written for Scripture Union's Bible reading notes series *Closer to God*, including a series on "The Father Heart of God" in 2001 and on the book of 2 Timothy in 2004. Her first book in a series for New Wine Press, *Expecting God to Speak to You!* was released in 2005, which was followed by *Letting God Speak Through You* in 2006 and *Encountering God* in 2007.

Tracy now regularly teaches at workshops, church weekends and conferences that she and Marilyn lead together. Some of the areas she teaches on are: prophetic prayer and ministry, listening to God, prophetic evangelism, intimacy with God, the Father heart of God, breaking out of loneliness, overcoming fear and anxiety, and becoming the true Body of Christ.

For Further Information

If you would like Tracy to speak at your church or if you would like more information about Tracy and Marilyn Baker Ministries, please contact:

Marilyn Baker Ministries
PO Box 393
Tonbridge
Kent
TN9 9AY

Tel: 08707 501720
Email: info@marilynbakerministries.org
Web: www.marilynbakerministries.org

BY THE SAME AUTHOR

Expecting God to Speak to You!
ISBN 978-1-903725-41-2
£5.99

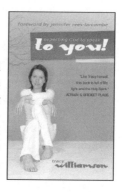

With many illustrations, personal stories and practical suggestions, Tracy Williamson helps us to tune in to God's voice of love and hear Him speaking in a variety of ways and circumstances. Readers will be amazed at how God will speak into all areas of their lives – not just those areas they consider to be "big" or "important". This book will revitalize your prayer life!

Letting God Speak Through You
ISBN 978-1-903725-49-8
£5.99

An ideal companion to Tracy's first book this deals with hearing God in order to speak encouragement and life to others. With great wisdom and sensitivity Tracy explains how to receive and handle prophetic words or words of knowledge, and helps the reader to avoid common pitfalls when sharing these words with others.

Encountering God
ISBN 978-1-903725-93-1

£5.99

This book is a fellow traveller's guide to the joy of discovering God afresh. The teaching in every chapter focuses on a key aspect of our relationship with God and shows how we can develop life-changing encounters with Him. The practical exercises and illustration will not only inform the reader but help them to encounter God for themselves.

Recommended Reading

For more in-depth study of some of the issues raised in this book I would recommend the following titles, all of which I have read and been blessed by. This is not an exhaustive list, just a few suggestions!

Live for a Change, Francis Dewar (Darton, Longman and Todd)
Waking the Dead, John Eldredge (Thomas Nelson Publishers)
God Is Closer Than You Think, John Ortberg (Zondervan)
Supernatural Breakthrough, Rachel Hickson (New Wine Press)
Abba's Child, Brennan Manning (Navpress)
The Supernatural Ways of Royalty, Kris Vallotton and Bill Johnson (Destiny Image Publishers)
Free to Be Me, Neva Coyle (Kingsway Publications)

We hope you enjoyed reading this New Wine book.
For details of other New Wine books
and a range of 2,000 titles from other
Word and Spirit publishers visit our website:
www.newwineministries.co.uk
email: newwine@xalt.co.uk